The Gospel of Yeshua Christ According To

MARK

'For The People'

Edition 01-Revision 05

Victor Robert Farrell

The New Separatist Bible
All current
Contact & Sales Information
Can be found at
www.NewSeparatistBible.com

The Gospel of
Yeshua Christ
According To
MARK
'For The People'

ISBN Number 978-1-910686-60-7

First published in this format

March 2017 by WhisperingWord

All current contact and sales information can be found at

www.TheNewSeparatists.com

Printed in The United Kingdom

for

WhisperingWord Ltd.

The Gospel of Yeshua Christ According To

MARK

'For The People'

WELCOME & SOME GOOD NEWS FOR YOU

The Gospel is the good news brought you by the God-man, Yeshua Christ, the Son of God. Your Creator, YHWH, has put His laws for this life and life eternal in His holy Word the Bible, in the heavens, and in your heart. These ten words, these ten commandments are as follows:

1. I am YHWH your God, …You shall have no other gods before me.

2. You shall not make to you any graven image, or any likeness of anything that is in heaven above, or that is in the earth beneath, or that is in the water under the earth, you shall not bow down yourself to them, nor serve them, for I YHWH your God am a jealous God, visiting the iniquity of the fathers upon the children to the third and fourth generation of them that hate Me; And shewing mercy to thousands of them that love Me, and keep My commandments.

3. You shall not take the name of YHWH your God in vain; for YHWH will not hold him guiltless that takes His name in vain.

4. Remember the Sabbath day, to keep it holy. Six days shall you labour, and do all your work, But the seventh day is the Sabbath of YHWH your God, in it you shall not do any work, you, nor your son, nor your daughter, your manservant, nor your maidservant, nor your cattle, nor your stranger that is within your gates, For in six days YHWH made heaven and earth, the sea, and all is in them, and rested the seventh day, wherefore YHWH blessed the Sabbath day, and hallowed it.

5. Honour your father and your mother, that your days may be long upon the land which YHWH your God gives you.

6. You shall not murder.

7. You shall not commit adultery.

8. You shall not steal.

9. You shall not bear false witness against your neighbour.

10. You shall not covet your neighbour's house, you shall not covet your neighbour's wife, nor his manservant, nor his maidservant, nor his ox, nor his donkey, nor anything that is your neighbour's.

OK. First the bad news.

Yeshua, the only begotten Son of YHWH tells us that keeping these ten commands are a matter of the heart, and it is there where they are kept and broken, and so much so, that Yeshua said if a man were even to look with lust in their heart at another man's wife, then that man has committed adultery. All people, have broken these ten words. All people have sinned and come short of the glory of God. God is holy, and there is nothing imperfect in His heaven. Therefore, because of the practical and heart-breaking of any of these ten commands, all people are condemned to hell and lost forever.

Now the very worst of news. This can't be fixed by you.

No amount of good works can make good our sins. No amount of religious rite, can make good our sins, No amount of prayerful intercession or personal sacrifice can make good our sins. We are lost, utterly and totally. The justice and the demand of these broken laws are your eternal death.

NOW THE GOOD NEWS!

Yeshua, the eternal Son of God, clothed Himself in a body and fully became a man, even a perfect human being. Thus, being fully God and fully human, He took the penalty of Your sin, that being death, and paid for it with His own death and now can grant Eternal life to anyone and everyone who comes to Him to ask for forgiveness. This is the Gospel of Yeshua Christ. Only Christianity offer forgiveness of sins through the death of someone else.

This is the word of faith which we preach; That if you shall confess with your mouth the Lord Yeshua, and shall believe in your heart that God has raised Him from the dead, you shall be saved. For with the heart man believes to righteousness; and with the mouth confession is made to salvation. For the Scripture said, 'Whoever believes on Him shall not be ashamed. For there is no difference between the Jew and the Greek, for the same Lord over all is rich to all that call upon Him. For whoever shall call upon the name of the Lord shall be saved. (Romans 10:9-13 NSB)

Rev. Victor Robert Farrell, May **2017**, England.

A PRAYER TO RECEIVE FORGIVENESS
AND LIFE ETERNAL

"Almighty God,

Thank you for sending Your Son to die for sinners just like me.

I believe that He died in my place and took the consequences of my rebellion against You upon Himself.

I am amazed, and so thankful that He suffered the punishment I deserved so that I don't have to.

I am sorry for the wrong I that have done and want to turn from it.

After being crucified for my sin, I believe that Jesus came back to life to prove that He had beaten both sin and death itself, and also to give me new life. This new life I now gratefully receive.

Therefore, please make right my relationship with You O God and send me Your Holy Spirit and let me know that I am forgiven and am Yours forever, and then my Holy Father, transform me from within.

Amen."

Let us know if you have prayed this prayer, and we can rejoice with you and help you achieve the destiny which God has for you!

Email us at vr@66Books.tv

Meet with other believers online at www.66Bible.Church

Bless you!

PREFACE

I am Pastor, Rev. Victor Robert Farrell, and the compiler of this confluence Bible which I call, the New Separatist Bible.

This is merely one of the 66Books which constitute the whole of the Holy Bible and it is the Gospel of Yeshua Christ according to St. Mark.

I love the Gospel of Mark because it is a simple Tabloid Headline Gospel. It gets straight to the point and is very easy reading. You are going to love it.

The purpose of presenting to you the Gospel according to St. Mark from the NSB is simply to introduce you to the greatness of Yeshua Christ the eternal and only begotten Son of God made flesh to die for You, crucified and raised from the dead for sinners like me and you that we might receive forgiveness, adoption into His family and life eternal!

Believe! Be saved! Enjoy!

Rev. Victor Robert Farrell, March **2017**, England.

AN BRIEF INTRODUCTION TO THE NEW SEPARATIST BIBLE (NSB)

The New Separatist's Bible (NSB) is a 'Confluence Bible,' and is rooted mainly in the Pure Cambridge Edition of the 1611 King James Authorized Version and shaped by the 1560 AND 1599 Geneva Bibles and 21st century English. It is, therefore, a confluence of these three great rivers, the Authorized Version, the Geneva Bible and modern English. Therefore, the NSB is NOT a translation, it is a confluence. As it brings together these rivers of translation into the 21st century, it is very happily NOT politically correct and NOT gender neutral.

So, just what is the NSB?

The NSB is a Bible is produced with a view to the Non-Christian. It is, therefore, one of a few 'Read & Learn' Bibles rather than a study Bible, and this learning is enabled by the very simple use of copious sub-headings, each rightly dividing the Scripture text into meaningful and instructively headed portions.

In this confluence Bible, I have also decided to use the Hebrew form of Jesus, 'Yeshua' for Son of God, and for the name of God our Father, instead of 'LORD' or 'Jehovah,' I have chosen to use the Holy Name of YHWH.

Finally, in this confluence NSB, I hope to have retained some of the majesty of language presented in these ancients translations rooted in the received text and with this confluence of compilation I have also tried to fully retain that great 'difference' that is, that great 'otherness' of the received Biblical text, as expressed in the 1560 & 1599 Geneva Bibles and especially the 1611 King James Authorized Version.

Finally, please note that this confluence called the NSB is in British English.

JUST A HUCKSTER

Some young preacher will study until he has to get thick glasses to take care of his failing eyesight because he has an idea he wants to become a famous preacher. HE'S JUST A HUCKSTER buying selling and getting gain. They will ordain him and he will be known as Reverend and if he writes a book, they will make him a doctor. And he will be known as Doctor; but he's still a huckster buying and selling and getting gain.

***And when the Lord comes back,
HE will drive him out of the temple
along with the other cattle.***

A.W. Tozer

(from 'Tozer on Christian Leadership,' compiled by Ron Eggert)

John 3:30 He must increase
but I must decrease.

STILL LOOKING

Wise men speak of trees
From the Cedar to the Hyssop
Springing from the wall
From the Aspen to the Alder
Beside the water fall

Wise men speak of animals of creeping things and fish
Of birds and bees and smooth black cats
That lap the dainty dish

Wise men sing of love and capture moments in a jar
Wise men suck the juice of days
Wise men shop at Spar!

Wise men count the fallen ticks
Of old clocks running down
Wise men number muscles
That help create the frown

Wise men follow after
Wise men follow far
Wise men seek the Savior still
Beneath the wandering star

1 Kings 4:33 Also he spoke of trees, from the cedar tree of Lebanon even to the hyssop that springs out of the wall; he spoke also of animals, of birds, of creeping things, and of fish.

The Old 100th!

All people that on earth do dwell,
Sing to the Lord with cheerful voice.
Him serve with fear, His praise out tell;
Come you before Him and rejoice.

The Lord, you know, is God indeed;
Without our aid He did us make;
We are His folk, He does us feed,
And for His sheep He does us take.

O enter then His gates with praise;
Approach with joy His courts to;
Praise, laud, and bless His name always,
For it is seemly so to do.

For why? the Lord our God is good;
His mercy is forever sure;
His truth at all times firmly stood,
And shall from age to age endure.

To Father, Son and Holy Spirit,
The God whom Heaven and earth adore,
From men and from the angel host
Be praise and glory evermore.

From 'Fourscore and Seven Psalms of David'
(Geneva, Switzerland: [1561]); attributed to William Kethe

CONTENTS

THE GOSPEL ACCORDING TO MARK

- *Total Original KJV Words | 15,166*
- *The 23rd Biggest Book in The Bible*
- *Total Verses | 678*
- *Total Chapters | 16*
- *This is the 41st Book of the Bible.*

Mark is written by John-Mark, the nephew of Barnabas, who failed miserably in the eyes of Paul when he 'lost his bottle' and deserted them at Perga on the first missionary journey.

Like Peter, John Mark got his act together after his fall. Indeed, many theologians believe that Mark was a disciple of Peter and got much of his information and active action lifestyle and method of communication, right from him.

Mark certainly gets straight to the point in his writing; he's a tabloid head-liner, and consequently, Mark is an 'ACTION' Gospel, and McGee says that, 'Mark was written by a busy man for busy people about a busy Person.'

So, Mark is all about headline action and deeds of daring and wonder, and all their associated emotions, and as John is his Hebrew name, Mark, being his Roman name, is emblematic of the primary audience to whom he is writing, - and you know the last human being to speak in this Gospel of Mark is a Roman Centurion speaking about Yeshua saying,

"TRULY THIS MAN WAS THE SON OF GOD."

(Mark 15,39 NSB)

| MARK | 41 of 66 |

CHAPTER 1

THE beginning of the Gospel of Yeshua Christ, the Son of God;

JOHN THE BAPTIST PREPARES THE WAY FOR YESHUA

(Mark 1:2-8)

² As it is written in the prophets,

"Behold, I send my messenger before Your face, who shall prepare Your way before You.
³ *The voice of one crying in the wilderness, Prepare you the way of the Lord, make His paths straight!"*

⁴ John was in the wilderness and baptized and preached the baptism of repentance for the remission of sins.

⁵ And there went out to him all the land of Judea, and they of Jerusalem, and were all baptized by him in the river Jordan, confessing their sins.

⁶ And John was clothed with camel's hair, and with a loincloth made of skin; and he ate locusts and wild honey;

⁷ And he preached, saying,

"There comes One after me who is mightier than I, whose sandal strap I am not worthy to stoop down and loose.

⁸ *I indeed have baptized you with water, but He shall baptize you with the Holy Spirit."*

GOD THE FATHER AFFIRMS THE BAPTISM OF YESHUA

(Mark 1:9-11)

⁹ And it came to pass in those days, that Yeshua came from Nazareth of Galilee, and was baptized by John in Jordan.

¹⁰ And straight away coming up out of the water, he saw the heavens ripped apart, and the Spirit like a dove descending upon Him,

¹¹ And there came a voice from heaven, saying,

"You are my beloved Son, in whom I am well pleased."

YESHUA SMOKES OUT THE DEVIL!

(Mark 1,12,13)

¹² And immediately the Spirit drove Him into the wilderness.

13 And He was there in the wilderness forty days, tempted by Satan; and was with the wild animals; and the angels ministered to Him.

YESHUA, VICTORIOUS OVER SATAN, NOW BEGINS HIS PUBLIC MINISTRY

(Mark 1:14,15)

14 Now after that John was put in prison, Yeshua came into Galilee, preaching the Gospel of the kingdom of God,

15 And saying,

"The time is fulfilled, and the kingdom of God is at hand, repent you, and believe the Gospel."

YESHUA, BEGINS TO GET HIS TEAM TOGETHER

(Mark 1:16-22)

16 Now as He walked by the sea of Galilee, He saw Simon and Andrew his brother casting a net into the sea, for they were fishermen.

17 And Yeshua said to them,

"Follow Me, and I will make you into fishermen of men."

18 And straight away they forsook their nets, and followed him.

19 And when He had gone a little further there, He saw James the son of Zebedee, and John his brother, who also were in the ship mending their nets.

20 And straight away He called them, and they left their father Zebedee in the ship with the hired servants, and went after Him.

21 And they went into Capernaum; and straight away on the Sabbath day He entered into the synagogue, and taught.

22 And they were astonished at His doctrine, for He taught them as one that had authority, and not as the scribes.

YESHUA & HIS AUTHORITY OVER STINKING-SPIRITS

(Mark 1:23-28)

23 And there was in their synagogue a man with a stinking-spirit; and he cried out,

24 Saying,

"Let us alone! What have we to do with You, Yeshua of Nazareth? Are You come to destroy us? I know you who You are, the Holy One of God."

25 And Yeshua rebuked him, saying,

"Hold your peace, and come out of him."

26 And when the stinking-spirit had torn him, and cried with a loud voice, he came out of him.

27 And they were all amazed, insomuch that they questioned among themselves, saying,

"What thing is this? What new doctrine is this? For with authority He commands even the stinking-spirits, and they obey him."

28 And immediately His fame spread abroad throughout all the region round about Galilee.

YESHUA & HIS FIRST PRIVATE HEALING

(Mark 1:29-31)

29 And straight away, when they were come out of the synagogue, they entered into the house of Simon and Andrew, with James and John.

30 But Simon's wife's mother lay sick of a fever, and before long, they tell Him about her.

31 And He came and took her by the hand, and lifted her up; and immediately the fever left her, and she ministered to them.

YESHUA & HIS FIRST PUBLIC HEALINGS

(Mark 1:32-34)

32 And in the evening, when the sun set, they brought to Him all that were diseased, and them that were possessed with demons.

33 And all the city was gathered together at the door.

34 And He healed many that were sick of different diseases, and cast out many demons; and did not allow the demons to speak, because they knew him.

YESHUA & HIS SOURCE OF PERSONAL POWER

35 And in the morning, rising up a great while before day, He went out, and departed into a solitary place, and there prayed.

36 And Simon and they that were with Him followed after Him.

37 And when they had found Him, they said to Him,

"All men seek for you."

YESHUA & HIS PERSONAL PRIORITY & POWER

(Mark 1:38,39)

38 And He said to them,

"Let us go into the next towns, that I may preach there also, for I came for this purpose."

39 And He preached in their synagogues throughout all Galilee, and cast out demons.

MR. BIG-MOUTH MAKES A MESS OF YESHUA'S MISSION

(Mark 1:40-44)

40 And there came a leper to Him, beseeching Him, and kneeling down to Him, and saying to Him,

"If You will, You can make me clean."

41 And Yeshua, moved with compassion, reached out His hand, and touched him, and said to him,

"I will; be clean!"

42 And as soon as He had spoken, immediately the leprosy departed from him, and he was cleansed.

43 And He strictly commanded him, and immediately sent him on his way;

44 And said to him,

"See you say nothing to any man, but go your way, show yourself to the priest, and offer for your cleansing those things which Moses commanded, for a testimony to them."

45 But he went out, and began to abundantly proclaim it, and to blaze abroad the matter, insomuch that Yeshua could no more openly enter into the city, but was outside in desert places, and they came to Him from every quarter.

CHAPTER 2

TAKING THE ROOF OFF A CROWDED HOUSE

(Mark 2:1-13)

AND again, after some days, He entered into Capernaum,; and it was reported abroad that He was in the house.

2 And straight away many were gathered together, insomuch that there was no room left to receive them, no, not even in the doorway, and He preached the Word to them.

3 And they came to Him, bringing one paralytic, carried by four.

4 And when they could not come near Him for the crowd, they uncovered the roof where He was, and when they had broken it up, they let down the bed in which the paralytic lay.

5 When Yeshua saw their faith, He said to the paralytic,

"Son, your sins are forgiven you."

6 But there were certain of the scribes sitting there, and reasoning in their hearts,

7 Why does this man speak blasphemies? Who can forgive sins but God alone?

8 And immediately when Yeshua perceived in His spirit that they so reasoned within themselves, He said to them,

"Why are you reasoning these things in your hearts?

9 *Whether is it easier to say to the paralytic, Your sins be forgiven you; or to say, Arise, and take up your bed, and walk?*

10 *But that you may know that the Son of man has power on earth to forgive sins,*

(He said to the paralytic,)

11 *I say to you, Arise, and take up your bed, and go your way into your house."*

12 And immediately he arose, took up the bed, and walked out in front of them all; insomuch that they were all amazed, and glorified God, saying,

"We have never seen anything like this!"

YESHUA RETURNS TO WIDE-OPEN SPACES

(Mark 2:13)

13 And He went out again by the sea side; and all the multitude came to Him, and He taught them.

YESHUA CALLS THE SCUM OF THE EARTH TO THE CAUSE OF HIS KINGDOM

(Mark 2:14)

14 And as He passed by, He saw Levi the son of Alphaeus sitting at the receipt of custom, and said to him,

"Follow me."

And he arose and followed Him.

THE DOCTOR HAS DINNER WITH THE DIRTY'S

(Mark 2:15-17)

15 And it came to pass, that, as Yeshua was eating in his house, many publicans and sinners also sat together with Yeshua and His disciples, for there were many, and they followed Him.

16 And when the scribes and Pharisees saw Him eat with publicans and sinners, they said to His disciples,

"How is it that he eats and drinks with publicans and sinners?"

17 When Yeshua heard it, He said to them,

"They that are whole have no need of the physician, but they that are sick, I came not to call the righteous, but sinners to repentance."

TELLING TIMES FOR FEASTING & TELLING TIMES FOR FASTING

(Mark 2:18-20)

18 And the disciples of John and of the Pharisees used to fast, and they came and said to Him,

"Why do the disciples of John and of the Pharisees fast, but Your disciples do not fast?"

19 And Yeshua said to them,

"Can the friends of the bridegroom fast, while the bridegroom is with them? As long as they have the bridegroom with them, they cannot fast.

20 *But the days will come, when the Bridegroom shall be taken away from them, and then shall they fast in those days.*

RETRO WILL RUIN THE NEW

(Mark 2:21,22)

21 *Also, no man sews a piece of new cloth on an old robe, else the new piece that filled it up takes away from the old, and the split is made worse.*

22 *And no man puts new wine into old bottles, else the new wine bursts the bottles, and the wine is spilled, and the bottles will be marred, but new wine must be put into new bottles."*

MAN IS THE REASON FOR THE SABBATH SEASON

(Mark 2:23-28)

23 And it came to pass, that He went through the corn fields on the Sabbath day; and His disciples began, as they went, to pluck the ears of corn.

24 And the Pharisees said to Him,

"Behold, why do they, on the Sabbath day, do that which is not lawful?"

25 And He said to them,

"Have you never read what David did, when he had need, and was hungry, he, and they that were with him?

26 *How he went into the house of God in the days of Abiathar the high priest, and ate the showbread, which is not lawful to eat except for the priests, and also gave to them which were with him?"*

27 And He said to them,

"The Sabbath was made for man, and not man for the Sabbath,

²⁸ *Therefore, the Son of man is also Lord of the Sabbath."*

CHAPTER 3

WORKING WONDERS WITH WELL-WITHERED PEOPLE

(Mark 3:1-5)

A ND He entered again into the synagogue; and there was a man there which had a withered hand.

² And they watched Him, whether He would heal him on the Sabbath day; that they might accuse him.

³ And He said to the man which had the withered hand,

"Step forward."

⁴ And he said to them,

"Is it lawful to do good on the Sabbath days, or to do evil? to save life, or to kill?"

But they held their peace.

⁵ And when He had looked round about on them with anger, being grieved for the hardness of their hearts, He said to the man,

"Stretch out your hand."

And he stretched it out, and his hand was restored whole as the other.

YESHUA REPULSES THE RELIGIOUS SELF-RIGHTEOUS

(Mark 3:6-8)

⁶ And the Pharisees went out, and straight away took counsel with the Herodians against Him, how they might destroy Him.

YESHUA ATTRACTS THE GROSSLY UNRIGHTEOUS

(Mark 3:7,8)

⁷ But Yeshua withdrew Himself with His disciples to the sea, and a great multitude from Galilee followed Him, and from Judea,

⁸ And from Jerusalem, and from Idumaea, and from beyond Jordan; and they about Tyre and Sidon, a great multitude, when they had heard what great things He did, came to him.

TOUCHING UNLOVELY EARS, & PLAGUED HEARTS,

(Mark 3:9,10)

⁹ And He spoke to His disciples, that a small ship should wait on Him because of the multitude, lest they should crush Him.

¹⁰ For He had healed many; insomuch that they pressed upon Him, as many as had plagues, so as to touch Him,

SILENCING THE STINKING SPIRITS

(Mark 3:11,12)

¹¹ And stinking-spirits, when they saw Him, fell down before Him, and cried, saying,

"You are the Son of God!"

¹² And He commanded them that they should not make Him known.

EMPOWERING THE TWELVE FOR MINISTRY

(Mark 3:13-19)

¹³ And He went up into a mountain, and called to Him whom He would, and they came to Him.

¹⁴ And He ordained twelve, that they should be with Him, and that He might send them out to preach,

¹⁵ And to have power to heal sicknesses, and to cast out demons,

¹⁶ And Simon He surnamed Peter;

¹⁷ And James the son of Zebedee, and John the brother of James; and He surnamed them Boanerges, which is, 'The sons of thunder!'

¹⁸ And Andrew, and Philip, and Bartholomew, and Matthew, and Thomas, and James the son of Alphaeus, and Thaddaeus, and Simon the Canaanite,

¹⁹ And Judas Iscariot, which also betrayed Him, and they went into an house.

FORMER FRIENDS TRY TO SECTION THE SAVIOUR

(Mark 3:13-19)

20 And the multitude came together again, so that they could not so much as eat bread.

21 And when His friends heard of it, they went out to lay hold on Him, for they said,

"He is beside himself!"

SATANIC SCRIBES SPREAD FAKE NEWS
(Mark 3:22-27)
22 And the scribes which came down from Jerusalem said,

"He has Beelzebub, and by the prince of the demons He casts out demons."

23 And He called them to Himself, and said to them in parables,

"How can Satan cast out Satan?

24 *And if a kingdom be divided against itself, that kingdom cannot stand.*

25 *And if a house be divided against itself, that house cannot stand.*

26 *And if Satan rise up against himself, and be divided, he cannot stand, but has an end.*

27 *No man can enter into a strong man's house, and spoil his goods, except he will first bind the strong man; and then he will spoil his house."*

BE VERY CAREFUL WHO YOU LIE ABOUT!
(Mark 3:28-30)
28 *"Truly I say to you, All sins shall be forgiven to the sons of men, whatever blasphemies they shall utter,*

29 *But he that shall blaspheme against the Holy Spirit will never be forgiven, but is in danger of eternal damnation."*

30 Because they said,

"He has a stinking-spirit."

YESHUA IDENTIFIES HIS TRUE &
INTIMATE FAMILY!
(Mark 3:31,32)
31 There came then His brethren and His mother, and, standing outside, sent to Him, calling Him.

32 And the multitude sat about Him, and they said to Him,

"Behold, Your mother and Your brethren outside are asking for You."

33 And He answered them, saying,

"Who is my mother, or my brethren?"

34 And He looked round in a circle at those who sat about Him, and said,

"Behold my mother and my brethren!

35 *For whoever shall do the will of God, the same is my brother, and my sister, and mother."*

CHAPTER 4

OPEN SPACES, NEW FACES, HIGH STAKES
(Mark 4:1,2)
AND He began again to teach by the sea side, and there was gathered to Him a great multitude, so that He got into a boat, and sat in it on the sea; and the whole multitude was on the land by the sea.

2 And He taught them many things by parables, and said to them in His teaching,

GROUND BREAKING TEACHING ON SOIL
TYPES
(Mark 4:3-9)
3 *"Listen up; Behold, there went out a sower to sow,*

4 *And it came to pass, as he sowed, some fell by the wayside, and the birds of the air came and devoured it up.*

5 *And some fell on stony ground, where it did not have much earth; and immediately it sprang up, because it had no depth of earth,*

6 *But when the sun was up, it was scorched; and because it had no root, it withered away.*

7 *And some fell among thorns, and the thorns grew up, and choked it, and it yielded no fruit.*

8 *And other fell on good ground, and did yield fruit that sprang up and increased; and brought out, some thirty, and some sixty, and some an hundred fold!"*

9 And He said to them,

"He that has ears to hear, let him hear."

THE DUAL PURPOSE OF PARABLES

(Mark 4:10-12)

10 And when He was alone, they that were around Him with the twelve asked Him about the meaning of the parable.

11 And He said to them,

"To you it is given to know the mystery of the kingdom of God, but to them that are outside, all these things are done in parables,

12 That seeing they may see,
and not perceive;
and hearing they may hear,
and not understand;
lest at any time they should be converted,
and their sins should be forgiven them."

THE PARABLE OF THE SOWER-
UNPACKED!

(Mark 4:13-20)

13 And He said to them,

"Don't you understand this parable? How then will you understand all the parables?

14 ¶ *The sower sows the Word.*

15 *And these are they by the wayside, where the Word is sown; but when they have heard, Satan comes immediately, and takes away the Word that was sown in their hearts.*

16 *And these are they likewise which are sown on stony ground; who, when they have heard the Word, immediately receive it with gladness;*

17 *And have no root in themselves, and so endure but for a time, afterward, when affliction or persecution arises for the Word's sake, immediately they are resentful.*

18 *And these are they which are sown among thorns; such as hear the Word,*

19 *And the cares of this world, and the deceitfulness of riches, and the lusts of other things entering in, choke the Word, and it becomes unfruitful.*

20 *And these are they which are sown on good ground; such as hear the Word, and receive it, and bear fruit, some thirtyfold, some sixty, and some an hundred."*

LIGHT IS FOR SHINING & FOR THE
SHOWING OF SECRETS

(Mark 4:21-23)

21 ¶ And He said to them,

"Is a candle brought to be put under a bushel, or under a bed? and not to be set on a candlestick?

22 *For there is nothing hid, which shall not be manifested; neither was anything kept secret, but that it should come to light.*

23 *If any man have ears to hear, let him hear."*

REWARDS FOR OPEN EARS

(Mark 4:24.25)

24 And He said to them,

"Take heed what you hear, with the same measure you use, it shall be measured to you, and to you that hear, shall more be given.

25 *For he that has, to him shall be given, and he that has not, from him shall be taken even that which he has."*

THE FOUR SEASONS OF THE KINGDOM OF
GOD

(Mark 4:26-29)

26 ¶ *And He said,*

"So is the kingdom of God, as if a man should cast seed into the ground;

27 *And should sleep, and rise night and day, and the seed should spring and grow up, he knows not how.*

28 *For the earth brings out fruit of herself;*

THE NEW SEPARATIST BIBLE 7

first the blade, then the ear, after that the full corn in the ear.

²⁹ *But when the fruit is brought out, immediately he puts in the sickle, because the harvest is here."*

THE RAPID GROWTH OF SMALL INSIGNIFICANT SEED
(Mark 4:30-32)

³⁰ And He said,

"To what shall we liken the kingdom of God? or with what parable shall we describe it?

³¹ *It is like a grain of mustard seed, which, when it is sown in the earth, is less than all the seeds that are in the earth,*

³² *But when it is sown, it grows up, and becomes greater than all herbs, and shoots out great branches; so that the birds of the air may lodge under the shadow of it."*

PARABLES –THE TIP OF THE TEACHING SPEAR
(Mark 4:33,34)

³³ And with many such parables He preached the Word to them, as they were able to understand it.

³⁴ But without a parable He did not speak to them. And when they were alone, He explained all things to His disciples.

THE NAUGHTY PUPPY IS CALLED TO HEAL
(Mark 4:35-41)

³⁵ And the same day, when the evening was come, He said to them, Let us cross over to the other side.

³⁶ And when they had sent away the multitude, they took Him along in the boat as He was. And there were also with Him other little boats.

³⁷ And there arose a great storm of wind, and the waves beat into the boat, so that it was now full.

³⁸ And He was in the stern of the ship, asleep on a pillow, and they woke Him up, and said to Him,

"Master, don't you care that we are being destroyed?"

³⁹ And He arose, and rebuked the wind, and said to the sea,

"Peace, be still!"

And the wind ceased, and there was a great calm.

⁴⁰ And He said to them,

"Why are you so fearful? How is it that you have no faith?"

⁴¹ And they feared exceedingly, and said one to another,

"What manner of man is this, that even the wind and the sea obey Him?"

CHAPTER 5

YESHUA THE LIGHT MAGNET FOR EVERY DARKNESS
(Mark 5:1-20)

AND they came over to the other side of the sea, into the country of the Gadarenes.

² And when He was come out of the boat, immediately there met Him out of the tombs a man with a stinking-spirit,

³ Who had his dwelling among the tombs; and no man could bind him, no, not with chains,

⁴ Because that he had been often bound with manacles and chains, and the chains had been picked apart by him, and the manacles broken in pieces, neither could any man tame him.

⁵ And always, night and day, he was in the mountains, and in the tombs, crying, and cutting himself with stones.

⁶ But when he saw Yeshua afar off, he ran and worshipped him,

⁷ And cried with a loud voice, and said,

"What have I to do with you, Yeshua, you Son of the Most High God? I charge you by God, that You torment me not."

8 For He said to him,

"Come out of the man, you stinking-spirit."

9 And He asked him,

"What is your name?"

And he answered, saying,

"My name is Legion, for we are many."

10 And he begged him much that he would not send them away out of the country.

11 Now there was there near to the mountains a great herd of swine feeding.

12 And all the demons begged him, saying,

"Send us into the swine, that we may enter into them."

13 And so Yeshua gave them leave. And the stinking-spirits went out, and entered into the swine, and the herd ran violently down a steep place into the sea, (they were about two thousand;) and were choked in the sea.

14 So those who fed the swine fled, and they told it in the city and in the country. And they went out to see what it was that had happened.

15 And they came to Yeshua, and saw the one who had been possessed by demons and had the legion, sitting and clothed and in his right mind. And they were afraid.

16 And those that saw it all told them how had happened to him that was possessed with the devil, and also concerning the swine.

17 And they began to plead with Him to depart out of their coasts.

18 And when He was come into the boat, he that had been possessed with the devil pleaded with Him that he might be with Him.

19 However, Yeshua did not permit him, but said to him,

"Go home to your friends, and tell them what great things the Lord has done for you, and how He has had compassion on you."

20 And he departed, and began to proclaim in Decapolis what great things Yeshua had done for him, and all men marvelled.

A FATHER PLEADS FOR YESHUA TO COME
AND HEAL HIS LITTLE LASS

(Mark 5:21-23)

21 And when Yeshua was passed over again by boat to the other side, many people gathered to Him, and He was near to the sea.

22 And, behold, there came one of the rulers of the synagogue, Jairus by name; and when he saw Him, he fell at His feet,

23 And begged him greatly, saying,

"My little daughter lies at the point of death, I pray you, come and lay Your hands on her, that she may be healed; and she shall live!"

OH IF I COULD BUT TOUCH THE HEM OF
HIS GARMENT

(Mark 5:24-34)

24 And Yeshua went with him; and many people followed Him, and crowded around Him.

25 And a certain woman, which had an issue of blood twelve years,

26 And had suffered many things of many physicians, and had spent all that she had, and was no better, but rather grew worse,

27 When she had heard of Yeshua, came in through the back of the crowd, and touched His robe.

28 For she said,

"If I may touch but his clothes, I shall be whole."

29 And straight away the fountain of her blood was dried up; and she felt in her body that she was healed of that affliction.

30 And Yeshua, immediately knowing in Himself that power had gone out of him, turned Him about in the crowd, and said,

"Who touched my clothes?"

31 And his disciples said to him,

"You can see the multitude crowding you, and you ask, Who touched me?"

32 And He looked round about to see her that had done this thing.

33 But the woman fearing and trembling, knowing what was done in her, came and fell down before Him, and told Him all the truth.

34 And He said to her,

"Daughter, your faith has made you whole; go in peace, and be whole, and healed of your affliction."

BELIEF MUST CONQUER BOTH FEAR AND FACT

(Mark 5:35-43)

35 While He was yet speaking, there came from the ruler of the synagogue's house certain which said,

"Your daughter is dead, why trouble the Master any further"

36 As soon as Yeshua heard the Word that was spoken, He said to the ruler of the synagogue,

"Be not afraid, only believe."

37 And He would not let any man follow Him, except Peter, and James, and John the brother of James.

38 And He comes to the house of the ruler of the synagogue, and sees the commotion, and them that wept and wailed greatly.

39 And when He came in, He said to them,

"Why all this disturbance and weeping? The little girl is not dead, but sleeping."

40 And they laughed Him to scorn. But when He had put them all out, He takes the father and the mother of the little girl, and them that were with Him, and goes in to where the little girl was lying.

41 And He took the little girl by the hand, and said to her,

"Talitha cumi;"

which is, being interpreted,

'Damsel, I say to you, arise.'

42 And straight away the little girl arose, and walked; for she was of the age of twelve years. And they were astonished with a great astonishment.

43 And He charged them strictly that no man should know what happened; and commanded that something should be given her to eat.

CHAPTER 6

UNBELIEF 'LIMITS' THE WORK OF YESHUA

(Mark 6:1-6)

AND He went out from there, and came into His own country; and His disciples followed Him.

2 And when the Sabbath day arrived, He began to teach in the synagogue, and many hearing Him were astonished, saying,

"From where has this man got these things? And what wisdom is this which is given to Him, that such mighty works are performed by His hands!

3 Isn't this the carpenter, the son of Mary, the brother of James, and Joseph, and of Jude, and Simon? and are not His sisters here with us? And they were offended at Him!

4 But Yeshua said to them,

"A prophet is not without honour, but in his own country, and among his own relations, and in his own house."

5 And He could do no mighty work there, except that He laid his hands upon a few sick folk, and healed them.

6 And He marvelled because of their unbelief. And He went round about the villages, teaching.

YESHUA COMMISSIONS THE TWELVE TO GO & PREACH

(Mark 6:7-13)

7 ¶And He called to Him the twelve, and began to send them out by two and two; and gave them power over stinking-spirits;

8 And commanded them that they should take nothing for their journey, save a staff only; no lunch bag, no bread, no money in their pocket,

9 But to wear sandals; and not put on two coats.

10 And He said to them, In whatever place you enter into an house, stay there till you depart from that place.

11 And whoever shall not receive you, nor hear you, when you depart there, shake off the dust under your feet for a testimony against them. Truly I say to you, It shall be more tolerable for Sodom and Gomorrah in the day of judgment, than for that city.

12 And they went out, and preached that men should repent.

13 And they cast out many demons, and anointed with oil many that were sick, and healed them.

THE ELITE ARE CONFUSED & CONFOUNDED

(Mark 6:14,15)

14 And king Herod heard of Him; (for His name was spread abroad,) and he said, That John the Baptist was risen from the dead, and therefore mighty works are wrought by Him.

15 Others said, That it is Elijah. And others said, That it is a prophet, or is one of the prophets.

16 But when Herod heard thereof, he said, It is John, whom I beheaded, he is risen from the dead.

HOW HEROD TOOK JOHN THE BAPTIST'S HEAD

(Mark 6:17-29)

17 For Herod himself had sent out and laid hold upon John, and put him in prison for Herodias' sake, his brother Philip's wife, for he had married her.

18 For John had said to Herod,

"It is not lawful for you to have your brother's wife."

19 Therefore Herodias had a quarrel against Him, and would have killed Him; but she could not,

20 For Herod feared John, knowing that he was a just and holy man, and reverenced him; and when he heard him, he obeyed many things, and heard him gladly.

21 And when a convenient day was come, Herod, on his birthday made a banquet for his lords, high captains, and chief estates of Galilee;

22 And when the daughter of the said Herodias came in, and danced, and pleased Herod and those that sat with him, the king said to the young woman,

"Ask of me whatever you will, and I will give it you."

23 And he swore to her,

"Whatever you shall ask of me, I will give it you, up to the half of my kingdom."

24 And she went out, and said to her mother,

What shall I ask?

And she said,

The head of John the Baptist.

25 And she immediately rushed back in to the king, and asked, saying,

"I want you to give me, as soon as possible, on a plate, the head of John the Baptist."

26 And the king was exceeding sorry; yet for his oath's sake, and for the sake of those who sat with him, he would not turn her demand down.

27 And immediately the king sent an executioner, and commanded his head to be brought, and he went and beheaded him in the prison,

28 And brought his head on a plate, and gave it to the young woman, and the young women gave it to her mother.

29 And when his disciples heard of it, they came and took up his corpse, and laid it in a tomb.

THE FIRST APOSTOLIC MISSION DEBRIEFING

(Mark 6:30)

30 And the Apostles gathered themselves together before Yeshua, and told Him all things, both what they had done, and what they had taught.

BATTLEFIELD ROTATION, REST & RELAXATION

(Mark 6:31,32)

31 And He said to them, Come apart into the wilderness, and rest a while, for there were many coming and going, so that they had no time even to eat.

32 And privately, by boat, they departed into a deserted place.

THE DESPERATE 'SHEEPLE,' DOG THE GREAT SHEPHERD

(Mark 6:33,34)

33 But the multitudes saw them departing, and many knew Him and ran there on foot from all the cities. They arrived before them and came together to Him.

34 And Yeshua, when He came out, saw a multitude of people, and was moved with compassion toward them, because they were as sheep not having a shepherd, and He began to teach them many things.

HEAVENLY PROVIZION FOR A BIG PICNIC IN THE PARK!

(Mark 6:35-44)

35 And when the day was almost over, His disciples came to Him, and said,

"This is a wilderness, and now it's getting very late,

36 *Send them away, that they may go into the country round about, and into the villages, and buy themselves bread, for they have nothing to eat."*

37 He answered and said to them,

"You give them something to eat."

And they said to Him,

"Shall we go and buy two hundred denarii worth of bread, and give them that to eat?"

38 He said to them,

"How many loaves have you got? Go and find out."

And when they found out, they said,

"Five, and two fishes."

39 And He commanded them to make everyone to sit down in many groups upon the green grass.

40 And they sat down in rows, by hundreds, and by fifties.

41 And when He had taken the five loaves and the two fishes, He looked up to heaven, and blessed, and broke the loaves, and gave them to his disciples to set before them; and the two fishes He divided among them all.

42 And they all ate, and were filled.

43 And they took up twelve baskets full of the fragments, and of the fishes.

44 And they that ate of the loaves were about five thousand men.

CROWD DISPERSAL–PRIVATE PRAYER & THE PERILS OF HARDNESS

(Mark 6:45-52)

45 And straight away He made His disciples to get into the boat, and go to the other side , even to Bethsaida, while He sent the people away.

46 And when He had sent them away, He departed onto a mountain to pray.

THE PERILS OF THE LACK OF RIGHT CONSIDERATION

(Mark 6:47-52)

47 And when the evening was come, the boat was in the middle of the sea, and He was alone on the land.

48 And He saw them rowing very hard indeed; for the wind was against them, and about the fourth watch of the night He comes to them, walking upon the sea, and would have passed them by.

49 But when they saw Him walking upon the sea, they supposed it had been a spirit, and screamed!

50 For they all saw Him, and were petrified.

And immediately He talked with them, and said to them,

"Calm down! It's me; don't be afraid."

51 And He went up to them into the boat; and the wind stopped, and they were utterly and immeasurably amazed!

52 For they had not truly considered the miracle of the loaves, for their heart was hardened.

THE PEOPLE'S CRUSHING CRUSADES OF MASS HEALINGS!

(Mark 6:53-56)

53 And when they had passed over, they came into the land of Gennesaret, and drew to the shore.

54 And when they were come out of the boat, straight away everyone knew it was Him,

55 And ran everywhere through that whole region and began to bring in beds those that were sick, wherever they heard He was.

56 And wherever He went, into villages, or cities, or the country, they laid the sick in the streets, and begged Him that they might touch as it were, just the hem of His robe,, and as many as touched Him were made whole.

CHAPTER 7

THE CRITICISMS OF THE GREAT UNWASHED

(Mark 7:1-5)

THEN came together to Him the Pharisees, and certain of the scribes, which came from Jerusalem.

2 And when they saw some of his disciples eat bread with defiled, that is to say, with unwashed, hands, they found fault.

3 For the Pharisees, and all the Jews, except that they wash their hands often, don't eat, holding hard to the tradition of the elders.

4 And when they come from the market, unless they wash, then they don't eat. And there are many other things which they have come to practice, like the washing of cups, and pots, brass utensils, and tables.

5 Then the Pharisees and scribes asked Him,

"Why don't Your disciples walk according to the tradition of the elders, but eat bread with unwashed hands?"

YESHUA TRASHES ALL ABSENT-HEART TRADITION

(Mark 7:6-13)

6 He answered and said to them,

"Well has Isaiah prophesied of you hypocrites, as it is written,

'This people honour Me with their lips, but their heart is far from Me.

7 *However, in vain do they worship Me, teaching for doctrines the commandments of men.'*

8 *For laying aside the commandment of God, you hold the tradition of men, as the washing of pots and cups, and many other similar things that you do.*

9 And He said to them,

"Full well you reject the commandment of God, so that you may keep your own tradition.

10 *For Moses said,*

'Honour your father and your mother;'

and,

'Whoever curses father or mother, let him be put to death,'

11 *But you say,*

If a man shall say to his father or mother, 'Whatever profit you might have received form me is ' Corban,' (that is to say, a gift to God,)

12 *then you allow him to do nothing, and no more for his father or his mother;*

13 *Making the Word of God of none effect through your tradition, which you have handed down. And many other similar things you do."*

PUBLIC WARNINGS OF INNER DEFILEMENT

(Mark 7:14-16)

14 ¶ And when He had called all the people to Him, he said to them,

"Listen up to me every one of you, and understand,

15 *There is nothing from without a man, that entering into him can defile him, but the things which come out of him, those are the things that defile the man.*

16 *If any man have ears to hear, let him hear."*

THE DUMMY-DISCIPLES GET A DOUBLING DOWN!

(Mark 7:17-23)

17 And when He left the people and went back into the house, His disciples asked Him concerning the parable.

18 And he said to them,

"Are you such simpletons as well? Do you not perceive, that nothing from the outside entering into a man, it cannot defile him;

19 *Because it doesn't enter into his heart, but into the stomach, and is eventually evacuated, thus purging out of him all food!"*

20 And He said,

"That which comes out of the man, that is what defiles the man."

21 *For from within, out of the heart of men, proceed evil thoughts, adulteries, fornications, murders,*

22 *Thefts, covetousness, wickedness, deceit, filthiness, wicked looks, blasphemy, pride, foolishness,*

23 *All these evil things come from within, and defile the man.*

YESHUA'S FAILED SECLUSION IN SIDON & A SYRO-PHOENICIAN SALVATION

(Mark 7:24-30)

24 And from there He arose, and went into the borders of Tyre and Sidon, and entered into a house, and would have wanted no one to know about it, but He could not be hid.

25 For a certain woman, whose young daughter had a stinking-spirit, heard of Him, and came and fell at his feet,

26 The woman was a Greek, a Syrophenician by nation; and she begged Him that He would cast out the devil from her daughter.

27 But Yeshua said to her,

"Let the children first be filled, for it is not appropriate to take the children's bread, and to cast it to the dogs."

28 And she answered and said to Him,

"Yes, Lord, yet the dogs under the table eat of the children's crumbs.

29 And He said to her,

"For this saying go your way; the devil is gone out of your daughter."

30 And when she was come to her house, she found the devil departed! And her daughter laid upon the bed.

THE DEAF & DUMB GET HEALED IN DECAPOLIS!

(Mark 7:31-37)

31 And again, departing from the coasts of Tyre and Sidon, He came to the sea of Galilee, through the middle of the coasts of Decapolis.

32 And they brought to Him one that was deaf, and had an impediment in his speech; and they implored Him put His hand upon Him.

33 And He took him aside from the multitude, and put His fingers into His ears, and He spat, and touched his tongue;

34 And looking up to heaven, He sighed, and said to him,

"Ephphatha,"

that is, 'Be opened.'

35 And straight away his ears were opened, and the cord of his tongue was loosed, and he spoke clearly.

³⁶ And He commanded them that they should tell no man, but the more he commanded them, the more they abundantly proclaimed it;

³⁷ And were overwhelmingly astonished, saying,

"He has done all things well, He makes both the deaf to hear, and the dumb to speak."

CHAPTER 8

NO 15 MINUTE TALK HERE! JUST DAYS OF DOCTRINE WITH NO DOUGHNUTS!

(Mark 8:1-9)

IN those days the multitude being very great, and having nothing to eat, Yeshua called his disciples to Himself, and said to them,

² *"I have compassion on the multitude, because they have now been with me three days, and have had nothing to eat,*

³ *And if I send them away fasting to their own houses, they will faint by the way, for many of them came from far away.*

⁴ And His disciples answered Him,

"From where can a man satisfy these men with bread here in the wilderness?"

⁵ And He asked them,

"How many loaves have you?"

And they said,

"Seven."

⁶ And He commanded the people to sit down on the ground, and He took the seven loaves, and gave thanks, and broke them, and gave them to His disciples to set before them; and they did set them before the people.

⁷ And they had a few small fishes, and He blessed, and commanded to set them also before them.

⁸ So they ate, and were filled, and they took up seven baskets of fragments left over.

⁹ And those that had eaten were about four thousand, and He sent them away.

PHARISEES FREEZE YESHUA OUT OF THE REGION

(Mark 8:1-9)

¹⁰ And straight away He entered into a boat with his disciples, and came into the regions of Dalmanutha.

¹¹ And the Pharisees came out, and began to dispute with Him, seeking from Him a sign from heaven, tempting Him.

¹² And He sighed deeply in his spirit, and said,

"Why does this generation seek after a sign? Truly I say to you, There shall no sign be given to this generation."

¹³ And He left them, and boarding a boat, again departed to the other side.

DUMMY DISCIPLES STILL LEAVE YESHUA IN DISBELIEF!!

(Mark 8:14-21)

¹⁴ Now the disciples had forgotten to take bread, neither had they in the boat with them more than one loaf.

¹⁵ And He warned them, saying,

"Take heed, beware of the leaven of the Pharisees, and of the leaven of Herod."

¹⁶ And they ruminated among themselves, saying,

'It is because we have no bread."

¹⁷ And when Yeshua became aware of it, He said to them,

"Why are you ruminating over having no bread? Do you neither see nor understand yet? Is your heart still hardened?

¹⁸ *Having eyes, don't you see? and having ears, don't you hear, and don't you remember?*

¹⁹ *When I broke the five loaves among the five thousand, how many baskets full of fragments did you gather up?"*

They said to him,

"Twelve."

20 *"And when the seven were distributed among the four thousand, how many baskets full of fragments did you gather up?"*

And they said,

"Seven."

21 And He said to them,

"How is it then that you do not understand?"

DOUBLE MIRACLE DEALS WITH 'THE UNDERSTANDING'

(Mark 8:22-26)

22 ¶ And He came to Bethsaida; and they brought a blind man to Him, and begged Him to touch him.

23 And He took the blind man by the hand, and led him out of the town; and when He had spit on his eyes, and put his hands upon him, He asked him if He saw anything?

24 And he looked up, and said,

"I see men as trees, walking."

25 After that He put his hands again upon His eyes, and made him look up, and he was restored, and saw every man clearly.

26 And He sent him away to his house, saying,

"Neither go into the town, nor tell this to anyone in the town."

YESHUA INVESTIGATES IF HIS TEAM SEE WHO HE TRULY IS

(Mark 8:27-30)

27 And Yeshua and His disciples went out into the towns of Caesarea Philippi, and along the way He asked His disciples, saying to them,

"Who do men say that I am?"

28 And they answered,

"John the Baptist, but some say, Elijah; and others, one of the prophets."

29 And He said to them,

"But who do you say that I am?

And Peter answered and said to Him,

"You are the Christ."

30 And He commanded them that they should tell no man about Him.

YESHUA TELLS OF HIS COMING SUFFERING

(Mark 8:31)

31 And He began to teach them, that the Son of man must suffer many things, and be rejected by the elders, and by the chief priests, and scribes, and be killed, and after three days rise again.

A RETURN REBUKE LEAVES PETER FLOORED!

(Mark 8:32-34)

32 And He spoke about this openly. And Peter took Him aside, and began to rebuke Him.

33 But when He had turned around and looked at His disciples, He rebuked Peter, saying,

"Get you behind me, Satan, for you are not mindful of the things of God, but of the things of men."

A CHARGE FOR HUMILITY, COURAGE & CONTINUANCE!

(Mark 8:34-38)

34 ¶ And when He had called the people and his disciples to Himself, He said to them,

"Whoever will come after Me, let him deny himself, and take up his cross, and follow Me.

35 *For whoever will save his life shall lose it; but whoever shall lose his life for My sake and the Gospel's, the same shall save it.*

36 *For what shall it profit a man, if he shall gain the whole world, and lose his own soul?*

37 *Or what shall a man give in exchange for his soul?*

38 *Whoever, therefore, shall be ashamed of Me and of My words in this adulterous and sinful generation; of him shall the Son of man also be ashamed, when He comes in*

the glory of his Father with the holy angels."

CHAPTER 9

(This verse really belongs at the end of Mark chapter 8)

EYES THAT SHALL SEE THE COMING
KINGDOM OF POWER!

(Mark 9:1)

A ND He said to them,

"Truly I say to you, That there are some of you that stand here, which shall not taste of death, till they have seen the kingdom of God come with power."

ON THE MOUNTAIN PEAK, YESHUA GIVES
THE INNER CIRCLE A PEEK INSIDE!

(Mark 9,2,3)

² And after six days Yeshua took with Him Peter, and James, and John, apart by themselves, and lead them up into an high mountain and He was transfigured before them.

³ And His clothes became shining, brilliantly white like snow; so as no launderer on earth can make them white.

REPRESENTATIVES OF THE LAW & THE
PROPHETS ACCOMPANY YESHUA

(Mark 9:4-6)

⁴ And there appeared to them Elijah with Moses, and they were talking with Yeshua.

⁵ And Peter responded and said to Yeshua,

"Master, it is good for us to be here, so let us make three tabernacles; one for you, and one for Moses, and one for Elijah."

⁶ For he did not know what to say; for they were very afraid.

YHWH GET'S THEM TO THE POINT OF IT
ALL

(Mark 9:7,8)

⁷ And there was a cloud that overshadowed them, and a voice came out of the cloud, saying,

"This is my beloved Son, listen to Him."

⁸ And suddenly, when they looked around, they saw no man any more, except Yeshua only along with themselves.

ELIJAH-THE MAN-THE SPIRIT-THE END-
TIME APPEARING

(Mark 9:9-13)

⁹ And as they came down from the mountain, He commanded them that they should tell no man what things they had seen, until the Son of man was risen from the dead.

¹⁰ And they kept that saying to themselves, questioning with one another just what the rising from the dead should mean?

¹¹ And they asked Him, saying,

"Why do the scribes say that Elijah must first come?"

¹² And He answered and told them,

"Elijah truly comes first, and restores all things; and as it is written of the Son of man, He must suffer many things, and be treated with contempt.

¹³ *But I say to you, That Elijah has indeed come, and they have done to him whatever they wanted, as it is written of him."*

YESHUA RESCUES HIS DISCIPLES FROM A
FAILURE TO DELIVER

(Mark 9:9-29)

¹⁴ And when He came to his disciples, He saw a great crowd around them, and the scribes questioning with them.

¹⁵ And straight away all the people, when they saw Him, were very excited, and running to Him greeted Him.

¹⁶ And He asked the scribes,

"What questions are you asking them?"

¹⁷ And one of the multitude answered and said,

"Master, I have brought to you my son, which has a dumb spirit;

18 *And wherever he takes him, he tears him, and he foams, and gnashes with his teeth, and pines away, and I spoke to your disciples that they should cast him out; and they could not.*

19 He answered him, and said,

"O faithless generation, how long shall I be with you? how long shall I put up you? bring him to Me."

20 And they brought him to Him, and when he saw him, straight away the spirit tore him; and he fell on the ground, and wallowed in foaming.

21 And He asked his father,

"How long ago since this came to him"

And he said,

"Since a child

22 *And often times it has cast him into the fire, and into the waters, to destroy him, but if You can do anything, have compassion on us, and help us."*

23 Yeshua said to him,

"If you can believe, all things are possible to him that believes."

24 And straight away the father of the child cried out, and said with tears,

"Lord, I believe; You help my unbelief!"

25 When Yeshua saw that the people came running together, He rebuked the stinking spirit, saying to him,

"You dumb and deaf spirit, I command you, come out of him, and enter no more into him."

26 And the spirit cried, and greatly convulsed him, and came out of him, and he looked as if he was dead; insomuch that many said,

"He is dead."

27 But Yeshua took him by the hand, and lifted him up; and he arose.

28 And when He came back into the house, His disciples asked Him privately,

"Why could not we cast him out?"

29 And He said to them,

"This kind can come out by nothing but prayer and fasting."

YESHUA FORCES THEM TO FACE THE FEAR OF HIS DEPARTURE

(Mark 9:30-32)

30 And they departed from there, and passed through Galilee; and He did not want anyone to know it.

31 For He taught His disciples, and said to them,

"The Son of man is delivered into the hands of men, and they shall kill Him; and after that He is killed, He shall rise the third day."

32 But they did not understand the saying, and were afraid to ask Him.

YESHUA PUTS THEM IN A DIVINE 'PECKING ORDER'

(Mark 9:33-37)

33 And He came to Capernaum, and being in the house He asked them,

"What was it that you disputed among yourselves on the road?"

34 But they kept quiet, for on the road they had disputed among themselves about who should be the greatest.

35 And He sat down, and called the twelve, and said to them,

"If any man desire to be first, the same shall be last of all, and servant of all."

36 And He took a child, and put him in the middle of them, and when He had taken him in his arms, He said to them,

37 *"Whoever shall receive one of these children in my name, receives Me, and whoever shall receive Me, receives not Me, but Him that sent Me."*

THE OUTER CIRCLE SHOULD BLESS THE INNER-WOE IF THEY DON'T!

(Mark 9:38-42)

38 ¶ And John answered him, saying,

"Master, we saw somebody casting out demons in Your name, and he doesn't

follow us, and we stopped him, because he does not follow us."

³⁹ But Yeshua said,

"Don't stop him! for there is no man which shall do a miracle in My name, that can soon afterwards speak evil of me.

⁴⁰ *For he that is not against us is on our side.*

⁴¹ *For whoever shall give you a cup of water to drink in my name, because you belong to Christ, truly I say to you, he shall not lose his reward.*

⁴² *And whoever shall offend one of these little ones that believe in me, it is better for him that a millstone were hanged about his neck, and he were cast into the sea."*

BE WHOLE-HEARTED- BE FULLY COMMITTED-BE A FANATIC!
(Mark 9:43-49)

⁴³ *"And if your hand causes you to sin, cut it off, it is better for you to enter into life maimed, than having two hands to go into hell, into the fire that never shall be quenched,*

⁴⁴ *Where their worm never dies, and the fire is not quenched.*

⁴⁵ *And if your foot causes you to sin, cut it off, it is better for you to enter limping into life, than having two feet to be cast into hell, into the fire that never shall be quenched,*

⁴⁶ *Where their worm never dies, and the fire is not quenched.*

⁴⁷ *And if your eye causes you to sin, pluck it out, it is better for you to enter into the kingdom of God with one eye, than having two eyes to be cast into hell fire,*

⁴⁸ *Where their worm never dies, and the fire is not quenched.*

⁴⁹ *For everyone shall be seasoned with fire, and every sacrifice shall be seasoned with salt.*

⁵⁰ *Salt is good, but if the salt has lost its saltiness, how will you season it? Have salt*

in yourselves, and have peace one with another."

CHAPTER 10

TEMPTED BY DIVORCE!
(Mark 10:1-5)

AND He arose from there, and came into the coasts of Judea on the other side of Jordan, and the people went out to Him again; and, as He was accustomed, He again taught them.

² And the Pharisees came to Him, and asked Him, tempting Him,

"Is it lawful for a man to divorce his wife?"

³ And He answered and said to them,

"What did Moses command you?"

⁴ And they said,

"Moses permitted us to write a bill of divorce, and to put her away."

⁵ And Yeshua answered and said to them,

"Because of the hardness of your heart he wrote you this regulation."

YHWH'S INVENTION AND TRUE INTENTION REGARDING MARRIAGE!
(Mark 10:6-9)

⁶ *But from the beginning of the creation God made them male and female.*

⁷ *For this cause shall a man leave his father and mother, and stick close to his wife;*

⁸ *And the two shall be one flesh, so then they are no more two, but one flesh.*

⁹ *What therefore God has joined together, let not man split apart."*

DISCIPLES ARE STUNNED AT THE SERIOUS SEVERITY OF DIVORCE!
(Mark 10:10-12)

¹⁰ And in the house His disciples asked Him again about this same matter.

¹¹ And He said to them,

"Whoever shall put away his wife, and marry another, commits adultery against her.

¹² *And if a woman shall put away her husband, and be married to another, she commits adultery."*

'RED OR YELLOW BLACK OR WHITE THEY ARE PRECIOUS IN HIS SIGHT!'

(Mark 10:13-16)

¹³ And they brought young children to Him, that He should touch them, and his disciples rebuked those that brought them.

¹⁴ But when Yeshua saw it, he was very displeased, and said to them,

"Suffer the little children to come to me, and forbid them not, for of such is the kingdom of God.

¹⁵ *Truly I say to you, Whoever does not receive the kingdom of God as a little child, he shall not enter into it."*

¹⁶ And He took them up in His arms, put his hands upon them, and blessed them.

ITS NOT ABOUT GETTING RICHES, BUT ABOUT GIVING THEM AWAY!

(Mark 10:17-27)

¹⁷ And when He was back on the road, there came one running, and kneeled before Him, and asked Him,

"Good Master, what shall I do that I may inherit eternal life?"

¹⁸ *And Yeshua said to him,*

"Why do you call me good? There is no one good except one, and that is, God.

¹⁹ *You know the commandments,*

'Do not commit adultery,
Do not kill,
Do not steal,
Do not bear false witness,
Do not defraud,
Honour your father and mother.'"

²⁰ And he answered and said to Him,

"Master, all these have I observed from my youth."

²¹ Then Yeshua beholding him loved him, and said to him,

"One thing you lack. Go on your way, sell whatever you have, and give to the poor, and you shall have treasure in heaven, and come, take up the cross, and follow Me."

²² And he was sad at that saying, and went away grieved, for he had great possessions.

²³ And Yeshua looked round about, and said to His disciples,

"How hard it is for them that have riches to enter into the kingdom of God!"

²⁴ And the disciples were astonished at His words. But Yeshua answered again, and said to them,

"Children, how hard is it for them that trust in riches to enter into the kingdom of God!

²⁵ *It is easier for a camel to go through the eye of a needle, than for a rich man to enter into the kingdom of God."*

²⁶ And they were utterly flabbergasted, saying among themselves,

"Who then can be saved?"

²⁷ And Yeshua looking upon them said,

"With men it is impossible, but not with God, for with God all things are possible."

NO ONE LOSES OUT WHEN THEY SACRIFICIALLY FOLLOW YESHUA

(Mark 10:28-31)

²⁸ Then Peter began to say to Him,

"Look now, we have left everything, and have followed You."

²⁹ And Yeshua answered and said,

"Truly I say to you, there is no man that has left house, or brethren, or sisters, or father, or mother, or wife, or children, or lands, for my sake, and the Gospel's,

³⁰ *But he shall receive an hundredfold now in this time, houses, and brethren, and sisters, and mothers, and children, and lands, with persecutions; and in the world to come eternal life.*

31 *But many that are first shall be last; and the last first."*

YESHUA MAKES THEM FACE THEIR FEARS AGAIN!

(Mark 10:32-34)

32 And they were on the road going up to Jerusalem; and Yeshua went before them, and they were amazed; and as they followed, they were afraid. And He took again the twelve, and began to tell them what things should happen to Him,

33 Saying,

"Behold, we are going up to Jerusalem; and the Son of man shall be delivered to the chief priests, and to the scribes; and they shall condemn Him to death, and shall deliver him to the Gentiles,

34 *And they shall mock Him, and shall scourge him, and shall spit on Him, and shall kill Him, and the third day He shall rise again."*

DISCIPLES- AS DUMB AS A BAG OF HAMMERS, STILL DON'T GET IT!

(Mark 10:35-40)

35 And James and John, the sons of Zebedee, went to Him, saying,

"Master, we want You to do for us whatever we shall desire.

36 And He said to them,

"What do you want Me to do for you?

37 They said to Him,

"Grant to us that we may sit, one on Your right hand, and the other on Your left hand, in Your glory."

38 But Yeshua said to them,

"You know not what you ask, can you drink of the cup that I drink of, and be baptized with the baptism that I am baptized with?"

39 And they said to him,

"We can!"

And Yeshua said to them,

"You shall indeed drink of the cup that I drink of; and with the baptism that I am baptized with, shall you be baptized,

40 *But to sit on My right hand and on My left hand is not Mine to give; but it shall be given to them for whom it is prepared."*

YESHUA EXALTS THE ATTITUDE OF A LAMB. THE LION WILL COME LATER!

(Mark 10:41-45)

41 And when the ten heard it, they got very upset with James and John.

42 But Yeshua called them to Him, and said to them,

"You know that they which delight to rule over the Gentiles dominate them; and their great ones exercise authority over them.

43 *But it shall not be so among you, but whoever will be great among you, shall be your minister,*

44 *And whoever of you will be the boss, shall become servant of all.*

45 *For even the Son of man came not to be ministered to, but to minister, and to give His life a ransom for many."*

BLIND-BART STOPS THE SON OF GOD ON THE ROAD TO JERICHO

(Mark 10:46-52)

46 Then they came to Jericho, and as He went out of Jericho with His disciples and a great number of people, blind Bartimaeus, the son of Timaeus, sat by the roadside begging.

47 And when he heard that it was Yeshua of Nazareth, he began to cry out, and say,

"Yeshua, you Son of David, have mercy on me."

48 And many told him to 'shut up!' But he cried out even more,

"You Son of David, have mercy on me!"

49 And Yeshua stood still, and commanded him to be called. And they call the blind man, saying to him,

"Cheer up and get on your feet; He is calling you."

⁵⁰ And he, casting away his robe, got up, and came to Yeshua.

⁵¹ And Yeshua responded and said to him,

"What do want Me to do for you?"

The blind man said to him,

"Lord, I want to receive my sight.

⁵² And Yeshua said to him,

"Go your way; your faith has made you whole."

And immediately he received his sight, and followed Yeshua in the way.

CHAPTER 11

"HEY HO, AWAY WE GO, RIDING ON A DONKEY"

(Mark 11:1-12)

AND when they came near to Jerusalem, to Bethphage and Bethany, at the mount of Olives, He sent out two of his disciples,

² And said to them,

"Go your way into the town opposite you, and as soon as you go in, you shall find a colt tied, upon which no man ever sat; untie him, and bring him.

³ *And if any man says to you, 'Why are you doing this? Answer that 'the Lord has need of him;' and straight away he will send him here."*

⁴ And they went on their way, and found the colt tied by the door outside in a place where two ways met; and they untied them.

⁵ And certain of them that stood there said to them,

"What are you doing untying the colt?"

⁶ And they replied to them just as Yeshua had commanded, and they let them go.

⁷ And they brought the colt to Yeshua, and threw their clothes on him; and He sat on him.

⁸ And many spread their clothes in the road, and others cut down branches off the trees, and strew them in the road.

⁹ And those that went before, and those that followed on, cried our, saying,

"Hosanna! Blessed is He that comes in the name of the Lord,
¹⁰ *Blessed be the kingdom of our father David, that comes in the name of the Lord, Hosanna in the highest!*

¹¹ And Yeshua entered into Jerusalem, and into the temple, and when He had looked around about upon all things, it was the evening, so He went out to Bethany with the twelve.

¹² And the next morning, when they were coming from Bethany, He was hungry,

THE CURSING OF THE FIG TREE-A PICTURE OF FRUITLESS ISRAEL

(Mark 11:13,14)

¹³ And seeing a fig tree afar off having leaves, He went to see if He might find anything on it, and when He came to it, He found nothing but leaves; for it was not the season for figs.

¹⁴ And Yeshua said to it,

"Let no man eat fruit of you ever again!"

And His disciples heard it.

THE CLEANSING OF THE TEMPLE-THE SEALING OF THE DEATH SENTENCE

(Mark 11:15-19)

¹⁵ And they came to Jerusalem, and Yeshua went into the temple, and began to cast out them that bought and sold in the temple, and overthrew the tables of the moneychangers, and the seats of them that sold doves;

¹⁶ And would not allow that any man should carry any wares through the temple.

¹⁷ And He taught, saying to them, I

"Is it not written,

'My house shall be called a house of prayer for all nations?'

but you have made it a den of thieves!"

¹⁸ And the scribes and chief priests heard it, and sought how they might destroy Him, for they feared Him, because all the people were amazed at His teaching.

¹⁹ And when evening time arrived, He went out of the city.

LESSONS IN CURSING AND BLESSING AND LESSONS IN FAITH !
(Mark 11:20-26)

²⁰ And in the morning, as they passed by, they saw the fig tree dried up from the roots.

²¹ Then Peter remembered and said to Him,

"Master, look at that! The fig tree which you cursed is withered away."

²² And Yeshua responding said to them,

"Have faith in God.

²³ *For truly I say to you, That whoever shall say to this mountain, 'Be removed, and be cast into the sea; and shall not doubt in his heart, but shall believe that those things which he said shall come to pass; he shall have whatever he said.'*

²⁴ *Therefore I say to you, Whatever things you desire, when you pray, believe that you receive them, and you shall have them!*

²⁵ *And when you stand praying, if you have anything against anyone, forgive them, so that your Father also which is in heaven may forgive you your trespasses.*

²⁶ *But if you do not forgive them, then neither will your Father which is in heaven forgive your trespasses."*

YESHUA REFUSES TO PLAY BALL WITH THE TOP RANKING ELITE!
(Mark 11:27-33)

²⁷ And they arrived again in Jerusalem, and as He was walking in the temple, there came to Him the chief priests, and the scribes, and the elders,

²⁸ And said to Him,

"By what authority are You doing these things? And who gave You this authority to do these things?"

²⁹ And Yeshua answered and said to them,

"I will also ask you just one question, and if you answer Me, I will tell you by what authority I do these things.

³⁰ *The baptism of John, was it from heaven, or of men? Answer Me."*

³¹ And they reasoned with themselves, saying,

"If we shall say from heaven; He will say, Why then did you not believe him?

³² **But if we say of men; they feared the people, for all men said of John, that that he was a indeed a prophet."**

³³ And they answered and said to Yeshua,

"We can't say."

And Yeshua answering said to them,

"Neither do I tell you by what authority I do these things."

CHAPTER 12

THE VICIOUS VINEDRESSERS- DROWNED LIKE RATS IN THEIR OWN FAT VATS!
(Mark 12:1-12)

AND He began to speak to them in parables.

"A certain man planted a vineyard, and surrounded it with a hedge, and dug a place for the wine vat, and built a tower, and leased it to vinedressers and went into a far country.

² *Now at vintage time he sent a servant to the vinedressers, that he might receive some of the fruit of the vineyard from the vinedressers.*

³ *And they caught him, and beat him, and sent him away empty.*

⁴ *And again he sent to them another servant; and they threw stones at him, and wounded him in the head, and treated him disgustingly and sent him away.*

5 *And again he sent another; and they killed him! And many others; beating some, and killing some.*

6 *Having yet therefore one son, his well-beloved, he at the last sent him to them, saying, 'They will respect my son.'*

7 *But those vinedressers said among themselves, 'This is the heir; come on, let's kill him, and the inheritance shall be ours.'*

8 *And they took him, and killed him, and threw him out of the vineyard.*

9 *What shall the lord of the vineyard do? He will come and destroy the vinedressers and will give the vineyard to others.*

10 *And have you not read this Scripture;*

The stone which the builders rejected is become the head of the corner,
   11 *This was the Lord's doing, and it is marvellous in our eyes?"*

12 And they sought to get Him, but feared the people, for they knew that He had spoken the parable against them, so they left Him, and went on their way.

THE 'TOE-RAGS' TEST YESHUA ABOUT TAXES!

(**Mark 12:13-17**)

13 ¶ And they sent to him certain of the Pharisees and of the Herodians, to catch Him out in his words.

14 And when they arrived, they said to Him,

"Master, we know that You are true, and care for no man, for you regard not the person of men, but teach the way of God in truth, Is it lawful to give tribute to Caesar, or not?

15 *Shall we give, or shall we not give?"*

But He, knowing their hypocrisy, said to them,

"Why are you tempting me? Bring me a denarius, that I may see it."

16 And they brought it. And He said to them,

"Whose is this image and superscription?"

And they said to him,

"Caesar's."

17 And Yeshua answering them said,

"Render to Caesar the things that are Caesar's, and to God the things that are God's."

And they marvelled at Him.

THE SADDUCEES SEXY CONUNDRUM!

(**Mark 12:13-27**)

18 *Then Sadducees, which say there is no resurrection came to Hi,; and they asked Him, saying,*

19 *"Master, Moses wrote to us, If a man's brother die, and leave his wife behind him, and leaves no children, that his brother should take his wife, and raise up seed to his brother.*

20 *Now there were seven brothers, and the first took a wife, and dying left no seed.*

21 *And the second took her, and died, neither left he any seed, and the third likewise.*

22 *And the seven had her, and left no seed, last of all the woman died also."*

23 *In the resurrection therefore, when they shall rise, whose wife shall she be of them? for the seven had her to wife.*

24 And Yeshua answering said to them,

"Are you not in error, because you know not the Scriptures, neither the power of God?

25 *For when they shall rise from the dead, they neither marry, nor are given in marriage; but are as the angels which are in heaven.*

26 *Now regarding the dead, did you not read in the book of Moses, how in the bush God spoke to him, saying, 'I am the God of Abraham, and the God of Isaac, and the God of Jacob?'*

27 *He is not the God of the dead, but the God of the living, you therefore are greatly mistaken!"*

THE SCRIBE WHO CAME CLOSE TO THE KINGDOM

(Mark 12:28-34)

²⁸ ¶ And one of the scribes came, and having heard them reasoning together, and perceiving that He had answered them well, asked him,

"Which is the first commandment of all?"

²⁹ And Yeshua answered him,

"The first of all the commandments is, 'Hear, O Israel; The Lord our God is one Lord,

³⁰ *And you shall love the Lord your God with all your heart, and with all your soul, and with all your mind, and with all your strength, this is the first commandment.'*

³¹ *And the second is this, 'You shall love your neighbour as yourself.' There is none other commandment greater than these."*

³² And the scribe said to him,

"Well, said Master, you have spoken the truth, for there is one God; and there is none other but Him.

³³ *And to love Him with all the heart, and with all the understanding, and with all the soul, and with all the strength, and to love his neighbour as himself, is more than all whole burnt offerings and sacrifices."*

³⁴ And when Yeshua saw that he answered discreetly, He said to him,

"You are not far from the kingdom of God."

And after that no man dared to ask Him any question.

YESHUA PRESENTS A GOB-STOPPING PUZZLE

(Mark 12:35-37)

³⁵ And, while He taught in the temple, Yeshua asked,

"How come the scribes say that Christ is the Son of David?

³⁶ *For David himself said by the Holy Spirit,*

'YHWH said to my Lord, Sit on my right hand, till I make your enemies your footstool.'

³⁷ *David therefore himself called him Lord; therefore where is his son?"*

And the common people gladly heard Him.

YESHUA MAKES NEW FRIENDS!

(Mark 12:38-40)

³⁸ ¶ And He said to them in His teaching,

"Beware of the scribes, which love to go around in long cloths, and love respectful greetings in the marketplaces,

³⁹ *And the top seats in the synagogues, and the best places at feasts,*

⁴⁰ *Who devour widows' houses, and for a pretence make long prayers, these shall receive greater damnation!"*

GOD'S MEASURE OF GIVING!

(Mark 12:41-44)

⁴¹ And Yeshua sat across from the treasury, and watched how the people put money into the treasury, and many that were rich put in much.

⁴² And there came a certain poor widow, and she put in two mites, which make a quadrans.

⁴³ And He called to Him His disciples, and said to them,

"Truly I say to you, that this poor widow has put more in, than all that have put into the treasury,

⁴⁴ *For all they put in out of their abundance; but she out of her need cast in all that she had, even all her living!"*

CHAPTER 13

THE TOPPLING OF THE TOTTERING TEMPLE!

(Mark 13: 1,2)

A ND as He went out of the temple, one of his disciples said to Him,

"Master, see what manner of stones and what buildings are here!"

² And Yeshua answering said to him,

"Do you see these great buildings? There shall not be left one stone upon another, that shall not be thrown down."

RECOGNIZING THE SIGNS OF THE TIMES:
FALSE MESSIAHS

(Mark 13: 3-6)

³ And as He sat upon the mount of Olives across from the temple, Peter and James and John and Andrew asked him privately,

⁴ *"Tell us, when shall these things be? And what shall be the sign when all these things shall be fulfilled?"*

⁵ And Yeshua answering them began to say,

"Take heed lest any man deceive you,

⁶ *For many shall come in My name, saying, 'I am Christ;' and shall deceive many.*

RECOGNIZING THE SIGNS OF THE TIMES:
WARS AND RUMOURS OF WARS

(Mark 13: 7,8)

⁷ *And when you shall hear of wars and rumours of wars, don't you be troubled, for such things must needs be; but the end shall not be yet.*

⁸ *For nation shall rise against nation, and kingdom against kingdom, and there shall be earthquakes in different places, and there shall be famines and troubles, these are the beginnings of sorrows.*

RECOGNIZING THE SIGNS OF THE TIMES:
HARD PERSECUTION

(Mark 13: 9-13)

⁹ ¶ *But watch out for yourselves, for they shall deliver you up to councils; and in the synagogues you shall be beaten, and you shall be brought before rulers and kings for my sake, for a testimony against them.*

¹⁰ *And the Gospel must first be proclaimed among all nations.*

¹¹ *But when they arrest you, and deliver you up, take no thought beforehand, neither premeditate what you shall speak,,*

but whatever shall be given you in that hour, that speak you, for it is not you that speak, but the Holy Spirit.

¹² *Now brother shall betray brother to death, and the father the son; and children shall rise up against their parents, and shall cause them to be put to death.*

¹³ *And you shall be hated of all men for my name's sake, but he that shall endure to the end, the same shall be saved.*

RECOGNIZING THE SIGNS OF THE TIMES:
THE ABOMINATION

(Mark 13: 14-20)

¹⁴ ¶ *But when you shall see the abomination of desolation, spoken of by Daniel the prophet, standing where it ought not, (let him that reads understand,) then let them that be in Judea flee to the mountains,*

¹⁵ *And let him that is on the housetop not go down into the house, neither go inside, to take anything out of his house,*

¹⁶ *And let him that is in the field not go back for his coat.*

¹⁷ *But woe to them that are with child, and to them that are breast feeding in those days!*

¹⁸ *And pray you that your flight be not in the winter.*

¹⁹ *For in those days shall be affliction, such as was not from the beginning of the creation which God created to this time, and never again.*

²⁰ *And except that the Lord had shortened those days, no flesh should be saved, but for the elect's sake, whom He has chosen, Hhe has shortened the days.*

RECOGNIZING THE SIGNS OF THE TIMES:
THE FALSENESS ALL!

(Mark 13: 21,22)

²¹ *And then if any man shall say to you, 'Look, here is Christ; or, look, He is there; don't believe him,*

²² *For false Christs and false prophets shall rise, and shall show signs and wonders, to seduce, if it were possible, even the elect.*

RECOGNIZING THE SIGNS OF THE TIMES:
THE FAILING HEAVENS!

(Mark 13: 23-25)

²³ *But take heed and look now, I have foretold you all things.*

²⁴ ¶ *But in those days, after that tribulation, the sun shall be darkened, and the moon shall not give her light,*

²⁵ *And the stars of heaven shall fall, and the powers that are in heaven shall be shaken.*

RECOGNIZING THE SIGNS OF THE TIMES:
THE CLOUDS OF GLORY!

(Mark 13: 26)

²⁶ *And then shall they see the Son of man coming in the clouds with great power and glory.*

RECOGNIZING THE SIGNS OF THE TIMES:
THE HARVEST ANGELS!

(Mark 13: 27)

²⁷ *And then shall He send his angels, and shall gather together His elect from the four winds, from the uttermost part of the earth to the uttermost part of heaven.*

RECOGNIZING THE SIGNS OF THE TIMES:
THE FIGGIE-PUDDING PARABLES!

(Mark 13: 27-31)

²⁸ *Now learn a parable of the fig tree; When her branch is yet tender, and puts out leaves, you know that summer is near,*

²⁹ *So you, in the same manner, when you shall see these things come to pass, know that it is near, even at the doors.*

³⁰ *Truly I say to you, that this generation shall not pass, till all these things be done.*

³¹ *Heaven and earth shall pass away, but My words shall not pass away.*

HIDDEN DATES DEMAND DISCIPLES BE
PACKED & READY TO GO!

(Mark 13: 32-37)

³² *But of that day and that hour knows no man, no, not the angels which are in heaven, neither the Son, but only the Father.*

³³ *Take note, watch and pray, for you don't know when that time will be.*

³⁴ *For the Son of man is like a man taking a long trip, who left his house, and gave authority to his servants, and to every man his work, and commanded the door keeper to keep watch.*

³⁵ *So, you also watch, for you do not know when the master of the house returns, in the evening, or at midnight, or at the cockcrowing, or in the morning,*

³⁶ *Unless, suddenly coming, he finds you sleeping.*

³⁷ *And what I say to you. I say to all, Watch!"*

CHAPTER 14

THE RISING OF THE 'PLOTAFOOT'

(Mark 14: 1,2)

AFTER two days it was the feast of the Passover, and of unleavened bread, and the chief priests and the scribes sought how they might sneakily take Him, and put Him to death.

² But they said,

"Not on the feast day, lest there be an uproar of the people."

THE BROKEN BOX OF BETHANY'S WHORE

(Mark 14: 3-9)

³ ¶ And being in Bethany in the house of Simon the leper, as He was eating, there came a woman having an alabaster box of 'ointment of spikenard,' very precious; and she broke the box, and poured it on His head.

⁴ And there were some that were internally indignant! And said,

"Why was this waste of the ointment made?

⁵ *For it might have been sold for more than three hundred denarii, and have been given to the poor."*

And they deeply criticized her.

6 And Yeshua said,

"Let her alone; why are you troubling her? she has done me a great service.

7 For you always have the poor with you, and whenever you want to, you may do them good, but Me you have not always.

8 She has done what she could, she is come beforehand to anoint my body for burying.

9 Truly I say to you, Wherever this Gospel shall be preached throughout the whole world, this also that she has done shall be spoken of for a memorial of her."

THE BROKEN BOX OF MONEY THAT FINALLY BROKE JUDAS
(Mark 14: 10,11)

10 And Judas Iscariot, one of the twelve, went to the chief priests, to betray Him to them.

11 And when they heard it, they were glad, and promised to give him money. And he sought how he might conveniently betray him.

PASSOVER PREPARATIONS
(Mark 14: 12-16)

12 And the first day of unleavened bread, when they killed the Passover, His disciples said to Him,

"Where do you want us to go to make preparations that You may eat the Passover?

13 And He sent out two of his disciples, and said to them,

"Go into the city, and there shall meet you a man carrying a pitcher of water, follow him.

14 And wherever he goes in, say to the good man of the house,

"The Master asks, 'Where is the guest room, where I shall eat the Passover with my disciples?'"

15 And he will show you a large upper room furnished and prepared, there make ready for us.

16 And His disciples went out, and came into the city, and found it as He had said to them, and they made ready the Passover.

17 And in the evening He came with the twelve.

THE BETRAYER BREAKS COVER
(Mark 14: 18-21)

18 And as they sat and ate, Yeshua said,

"Truly I say to you, One of you which eats with me shall betray me."

19 And they began to be sorrowful, and one by one to say to Him,

"Is it I?"

and another said,

"Is it I?"

20 And He answered and said to them,

"It is one of the twelve, that dips with me in the dish.

21 The Son of man indeed goes just as it is written of Him, but woe to that man by whom the Son of man is betrayed! It were better for that man if he had never been born."

THE BREAKING OF BREAD THE NEW COVENANT OF WINE
(Mark 14: 22-26)

22 ¶ And as they ate, Yeshua took bread, and blessed, and broke it, and gave it to them, and said,

"Take, eat, this is my body."

23 And He took the cup, and when He had given thanks, He gave it to them, and they all drank of it.

24 And He said to them,

"This is my blood of the new covenant, which is shed for many."

25 Truly I say to you, I will drink no more of the fruit of the vine, until that day that I drink it new in the kingdom of God."

26 ¶ And when they had sung a psalm, they went out into the mount of Olives.

YESHUA WARNS OF THE COMING RUMBLE & STUMBLE
(Mark 14: 27-31)

27 And Yeshua said to them,

"All of you shall be offended because of me this night, for it is written,

'I will strike the shepherd, and the sheep shall be scattered.'

²⁸ *But after that I am risen, I will go before you into Galilee."*

²⁹ But Peter said to Him,

"Although all shall be made to stumble, even so, I won't!"

³⁰ And Yeshua said to him,

"Truly I say to you, that this day, even in this night, before the cock crow twice, you shall deny me three times."

³¹ But he spoke even more vehemently,

"If I should die with you, I will not in any way deny You!"

In the same manner, so said them all.

A PRILE OF PERPLEXING PRAYER AND PETER'S PITIFUL SNORING

(Mark 14: 32-42)

³² And they came to a place which was named Gethsemane, and He said to his disciples,

"You sit here while I pray."

³³ And He took with Him Peter and James and John, and began to be very perplexed, and very heavy;

³⁴ And said to them,

"My soul is exceeding sorrowful to death, wait here, and watch."

³⁵ And He went forward a little, and fell on the ground, and prayed that, if it were possible, that the hour might pass from Him.

³⁶ And He said,

"Abba, Father, all things are possible to you; take away this cup from me, nevertheless not what I will, but what You will."

³⁷ And He returned, and found them sleeping, and said to Peter, Simon,

"You're sleeping! Couldn't you watch for one hour.

³⁸ *Watch and pray, lest you enter into temptation. The spirit truly is willing, but the body is weak."*

³⁹ And again He went away, and prayed, and spoke the same words.

⁴⁰ And when He returned, He found them asleep again, (for their eyes were heavy,) and anyway, they did not know what to say to Him.

⁴¹ And He came a third time, and said to them,

"Sleep on now, and take your rest, it is enough, the hour is come; behold, the Son of man is betrayed into the hands of sinners.

⁴² *Get up and let's go; for look now, he that betrays me is at hand."*

DAMNATIONS SEALED WITH A KISS

(Mark 14: 43-46)

⁴³ ¶ And immediately, while He was still speaking, here comes Judas, one of the twelve, and with him a great mob with swords and staves, from the chief priests and the scribes and the elders.

⁴⁴ And he that betrayed Him had given them a sign, saying,

"Whomsoever I shall kiss, that's Him; take Him, and lead Him away safely."

⁴⁵ And as soon as he arrived, he went straight away to Him, and said,

"Master, master;"

and kissed Him.

⁴⁶ ¶ And they laid their hands on Him, and took Him.

PETER LOSES HIS HEAD AND MALCHUS LOSES HIS EAR

(Mark 14: 47-49)

⁴⁷ And one of them that stood by drew a sword, and struck a servant of the high priest, and cut off his ear.

48 And Yeshua spoke to them and said,

"Are you come out to get me, like you would a thief, with swords and with staves to take me?

49 *Every day I was with you in the temple teaching, and you did not arrest me, but the Scriptures must be fulfilled.*

50 *'And they all forsook Him, and fled.'*

MARK–THE FIRST YELLOW-BELLIED CHRISTIAN STREAKER!

(Mark 14: 51,52)

51 And there followed Him a certain young man, having a linen cloth thrown around his naked body; and the young men laid hold on him,

52 And he left the linen cloth, and fled naked from them!

YESHUA SUFFERS BEFORE THE SANHEDRIN!

(Mark 14: 53-65)

53 And they led Yeshua away to the high priest, and with Him were assembled all the chief priests and the elders and the scribes.

54 And Peter followed Him from afar even into the palace of the high priest, and he sat with the servants, and warmed himself by the fire.

55 And the chief priests and all the council sought for witness against Yeshua to put Him to death; but found none.

56 For many bore false witness against Him, but their joint testimony did not agree.

57 And there arose certain of them, and bore false witness against Him, saying,

58 *"We heard him say, I will destroy this temple that is made with hands, and within three days I will build another made without hands."*

59 But neither did their testimony match up with each other's.

60 And the high priest stood up in the middle, and asked Yeshua, saying,

"Are you going to say nothing? What is it these me testify against you?

61 But He kept quit, and answered nothing. Again the high priest asked Him, and said to Him,

"Are you the Christ, the Son of the Blessed?"

62 And Yeshua said,

"I am, and you shall see the Son of man sitting on the right hand of power, and coming in the clouds of heaven."

63 Then the high priest ripped his clothes apart, and said,

"What need we of any further witnesses?

64 *You have heard the blasphemy, what do you think?"*

And they all condemned Him to be guilty of death.

65 And some began to spit on Him, and to cover his face, and to punch Him, and to say to Him,

"Prophesy!"

And the servants slapped Him with the palms of their hands.

PETER CURSES LIKE A SAILOR THEN CRIES LIKE A BABY!

(Mark 14: 66-72)

66 ¶ And as Peter was below in the palace, there came one of the servant girls of the high priest,

67 And when she saw Peter warming himself, she stared at him, and said,

"You were with Yeshua of Nazareth as well!"

68 But he denied it, saying,

"I don't know nor even understand, what you are talking about."

And he went out into the porch; and the cock crowed.

69 And the servant girl saw him again, and began to say to them that stood by,

"This is one of them."

70 And he denied it again. And a little after that , they that stood by said again to Peter,

"Surely you are one of them, for you are a Galilaean, and your speech confirms it!"

71 But he began to curse and to swear, saying,

"I do not know this man of whom you speak."

72 And the second time the cock crowed. And Peter remembered the Word that Yeshua said to him,

"Before the cock crows twice, you shall deny me three times."

And remembering that, he wept.

CHAPTER 15

YESHUA APPEARS BEFORE PILATE!

(Mark 15: 1-15)

A ND straight away in the morning the chief priests held a consultation with the elders and scribes and the whole council, and bound Yeshua, and carried him away, and delivered Him to Pilate.

2 And Pilate asked Him,

"Are You the King of the Jews?

And He answering said to him,

"You said it."

3 And the chief priests accused him of many things, but He never responded.

4 And Pilate asked Him again, saying,

"Are you going to answer anything? Look at how many things they accuse You of".

5 But Yeshua yet answered nothing; so that Pilate marvelled.

6 Now at that feast he released to them one prisoner, whoever they desired.

7 And there was one named Barabbas, which was bound along with the other insurrectionists, who had committed murder in the insurrection.

8 And the mob, shouting out loud began to want him to do as he had always done with them.

9 But Pilate spoke to them, saying,

"Do you want me to release to you the King of the Jews?"

10 For he knew that the chief priests had delivered Him out of envy.

11 But the chief priests stirred up people, that he should rather release Barabbas to them.

12 And Pilate spoke again and said to them,

"What then do you want me to do to Him whom you call the King of the Jews?"

13 And they cried out again,

"Crucify Him!"

14 Then Pilate said to them,

"Why, what evil has He done?"

And they cried out the more exceedingly,

"Crucify Him!"

15 ¶ And so Pilate, willing to appease the mob released Barabbas to them, and delivered Yeshua, when he had scourged Him, to be crucified.

YESHUA SUFFERS IN THE PRAETORIAN!

(Mark 15: 16-20)

16 And the soldiers led Him away into the hall, called Praetorian; and they called together the whole garrison.

17 And they clothed Him with purple, and platted a crown of thorns, and put it around his head,

18 And began to salute Him,

"Hail, King of the Jews!"

19 And they hit Him on the head with a reed, and spat on Him, and bowing their knees worshipped Him.

20 And when they had mocked Him, they took off the purple from Him, and put his

own clothes back on Him, and led Him out to crucify Him.

SIMON OF CYRENE CARRIES THE CROSS

(Mark 15: 21)

²¹ And they compelled Simon a Cyrenian, the father of Alexander and Rufus, as he was coming out of the country and passing by, to carry His cross.

THE KING OF THE JEWS IS NAILED, HAILED, AND THEN CURSED

(Mark 15:22-32)

²² And they brought Him to the place Golgotha, which is, being interpreted, The place of a skull.

²³ And they gave Him wine mingled with myrrh to drink, but He did not take it.

²⁴ And when they had crucified Him, they divided His clothes, casting lots for them, deciding what every man should take.

²⁵ And it was the third hour, and they crucified Him.

²⁶ And the superscription of His accusation was written over,

'THE KING OF THE JEWS.'

²⁷ And with Him they crucified two thieves; the one on His right hand, and the other on His left.

²⁸ And the Scripture was fulfilled, which said,

'And He was numbered with the transgressors.'

²⁹ And they that passed by railed at him, wagging their heads, and saying,

"Ah, You that destroys the temple, and builds it in three days,

³⁰ *Save yourself, and come down from the cross."*

³¹ In the same vein the chief priests also mocking said among themselves with the scribes,

"He saved others; Himself he cannot save.

³² *Let Christ the King of Israel come down from the cross, that we may see and believe.*

And they that were crucified with him reviled him.

THE DARKNESS OF THE DESERTING

(Mark 33-36)

³³ And when the sixth hour arrived, there was darkness over the whole land until the ninth hour.

³⁴ And at the ninth hour Yeshua cried with a loud voice, saying,

"Eloi, Eloi, lama sabachthani?"

which is, being interpreted,

"My God, my God, why have You forsaken Me?"

³⁵ And some of them that stood by, when they heard it, said,

"Look! He called Elijah."

³⁶ And one of them ran and filled a sponge full of vinegar, and put it on a reed, and gave Him it to drink, saying,

"Let Him alone; let us see whether Elijah will come to take Him down."

THE WAY TO THE FATHER IS OPENED WIDE THROUGH THE SACRIFICE OF THE SON OF GOD!

(Mark 15:37-39)

³⁷ And Yeshua cried with a loud voice, and gave up the ghost.

³⁸ And the veil of the temple was ripped in two from the top to the bottom.

³⁹ ¶And when the centurion, which stood over against him, saw that he so cried out, and gave up the ghost, he said,

"Truly this man was the Son of God."

THE WAITING AND WAILING WOMEN ALL WATCH ON!

(Mark 15:40,41)

⁴⁰ There were also women looking on from afar, among whom was Mary Magdalene, and Mary the mother of James the less and of Joseph, and Salome;

⁴¹ (Who also, when He was in Galilee, followed Him, and ministered to Him;) and there were many other women which came up with Him to Jerusalem.

JOSEPH WRAPS UP YESHUA AND LAYS HIS
PIERCED AND BROKEN BODY TO REST

(Mark 15:42-47)

⁴² And now when the evening arrived, because it was the preparation, that is, the day before the Sabbath,

⁴³ Joseph of Arimathaea, an honourable council member, which also waited for the kingdom of God, came, and went in boldly to Pilate, and ardently requested the body of Yeshua.

⁴⁴ And Pilate was amazed that He was already dead, and calling to him the centurion, he asked him whether he had been dead for a while?

⁴⁵ And when the centurion confirmed it, he gave the body to Joseph.

⁴⁶ And he bought fine linen, and took Him down, and wrapped Him in the linen, and laid him in a tomb which was cut out of a rock, and rolled a stone against the opening of the tomb.

⁴⁷ And Mary Magdalene and Mary the mother of Joseph took note of where He was laid.

CHAPTER 16

YESHUA IS RISEN FROM THE DEAD!

(Mark 16:1-8)

A ND when the Sabbath was past, Mary Magdalene, and Mary the mother of James, and Salome, had bought sweet spices, that they might come and anoint him.

² And very early in the morning the first day of the week, they came to the tomb at the rising of the sun.

³ And they said among themselves,

"Who shall roll away the stone from the door of the tomb for us?"

⁴ And when they looked, they saw that the stone was rolled away, for it was very great.

⁵ And entering into the tomb, they saw a young man sitting on the right side, clothed in a long white robe; and they jumped with fear.

⁶ And he said to them,

"Don't be afraid. You seek Yeshua of Nazareth, which was crucified, He is risen; He is not here, look at the place where they laid Him.

⁷ But go on your way, tell his disciples and Peter that He went before you into Galilee, and there shall you see Him, just as he told you."

⁸ And they went out quickly, and ran away from the tomb; for they were shocked and shaken, and they did not speak to anyone; for they were afraid.

YESHUA APPEARS TO MARY
MAGDALENE!

(Mark 16:9-11)

⁹ Now when Yeshua was risen early the first day of the week, He appeared first to Mary Magdalene, out of whom He had cast seven demons.

¹⁰ And as they mourned and wept, she went and told them that she had been with Him,.

¹¹ And they, when they had heard that He was alive, and had been seen by her, didn't believe it.

YESHUA, DISGUISED, GIVES TOW
DISCIPLES A SURPRISE!

(Mark 16:12,13)

¹² ¶ After that, He appeared in another form to two of them as they walked and went into the country.

¹³ And they went and told it to the remainder, but they did not believe them neither.

YESHUA DELIVERS A SCOLDING OF
UNBELIEF TO THE SORRY DISCIPLES!

(Mark 16:14)

¹⁴ ¶ Afterward He appeared to the eleven as they were eating, and scolded them about their unbelief and hardness of heart, because they did not believe them that had seen Him after He was risen.

YESHUA'S GREAT COMMISSIONING OF HIS DISCIPLES!

(Mark 16:15-18)

¹⁵ And He said to them,

"Go you into all the world, and preach the Gospel to every creature.

¹⁶ *He that believes and is baptized shall be saved; but he that does not believe shall be damned.*

¹⁷ *And these signs shall follow them that believe; In my name shall they cast out demons; they shall speak with new tongues;*

¹⁸ *They shall take up serpents; and if they drink any deadly thing, it shall not hurt them; they shall lay hands on the sick, and they shall recover."*

YESHUA'S ASCENSION INTO GLORY!

(Mark 16:19)

¹⁹ So then after the Lord had spoken to them, He was received up into heaven, and sat on the right hand of God.

THE DISCIPLE'S DO THE 'STUFF!'

(Mark 16:20)

²⁰ And they went out, and preached everywhere, the Lord working with them, and confirming the Word with signs following. Amen.

.

AFORE YE GO! GOOD NEWS FOR YOU!

The Gospel is the good news brought you by the God-man, Yeshua Christ, the Son of God. Your Creator, YHWH, has put His laws for this life and life eternal in His holy Word the Bible, in the heavens, and in your heart. These ten words, these ten commandments are as follows:

1. I am YHWH your God, …You shall have no other gods before me.

2. You shall not make to you any graven image, or any likeness of anything that is in heaven above, or that is in the earth beneath, or that is in the water under the earth, you shall not bow down yourself to them, nor serve them, for I YHWH your God am a jealous God, visiting the iniquity of the fathers upon the children to the third and fourth generation of them that hate Me; And shewing mercy to thousands of them that love Me, and keep My commandments.

3. You shall not take the name of YHWH your God in vain; for YHWH will not hold him guiltless that takes His name in vain.

4. Remember the Sabbath day, to keep it holy. Six days shall you labour, and do all your work, But the seventh day is the Sabbath of YHWH your God, in it you shall not do any work, you, nor your son, nor your daughter, your manservant, nor your maidservant, nor your cattle, nor your stranger that is within your gates, For in six days YHWH made heaven and earth, the sea, and all is in them, and rested the seventh day, wherefore YHWH blessed the Sabbath day, and hallowed it.

5. Honour your father and your mother, that your days may be long upon the land which YHWH your God gives you.

6. You shall not murder.

7. You shall not commit adultery.

8. You shall not steal.

9. You shall not bear false witness against your neighbour.

10. You shall not covet your neighbour's house, you shall not covet your neighbour's wife, nor his manservant, nor his maidservant, nor his ox, nor his donkey, nor anything that is your neighbour's.

OK. First the bad news.

Yeshua, the only begotten Son of YHWH tells us that keeping these ten commands are a matter of the heart, and it is there where they are kept and broken, and so much so, that Yeshua said if a man were even to look with lust in their heart at another man's wife, then that man has committed adultery. All people, have broken these ten words. All people have sinned and come short of the glory of God. God is holy, and there is nothing imperfect in His heaven. Therefore, because of the practical and heart-breaking of any of these ten commands, all people are condemned to hell and lost forever.

Now the very worst of news. This can't be fixed by you.

No amount of good works can make good our sins. No amount of religious rite, can make good our sins, No amount of prayerful intercession or personal sacrifice can make good our sins. We are lost, utterly and totally. The justice and the demand of these broken laws are your eternal death.

NOW THE GOOD NEWS!

Yeshua, the eternal Son of God, clothed Himself in a body and fully became a man, even a perfect human being. Thus, being fully God and fully human, He took the penalty of Your sin, that being death, and paid for it with His own death and now can grant Eternal life to anyone and everyone who comes to Him to ask for forgiveness. This is the Gospel of Yeshua Christ. Only Christianity offer forgiveness of sins through the death of someone else.

This is the word of faith which we preach; That if you shall confess with your mouth the Lord Yeshua, and shall believe in your heart that God has raised Him from the dead, you shall be saved. For with the heart man believes to righteousness; and with the mouth confession is made to salvation. For the Scripture said, 'Whoever believes on Him shall not be ashamed. For there is no difference between the Jew and the Greek, for the same Lord over all is rich to all that call upon Him. For whoever shall call upon the name of the Lord shall be saved. (Romans 10:9-13 NSB)

Rev. Victor Robert Farrell, May **2017**, England.

A PRAYER TO RECEIVE FORGIVENESS
AND LIFE ETERNAL

"Almighty God,

Thank you for sending Your Son to die for sinners just like me.

I believe that He died in my place and took the consequences of my rebellion against You upon Himself.

I am amazed, and so thankful that He suffered the punishment I deserved so that I don't have to.

I am sorry for the wrong I that have done and want to turn from it.

After being crucified for my sin, I believe that Jesus came back to life to prove that He had beaten both sin and death itself, and also to give me new life. This new life I now gratefully receive.

Therefore, please make right my relationship with You O God and send me Your Holy Spirit and let me know that I am forgiven and am Yours forever, and then my Holy Father, transform me from within.

Amen."

Let us know if you have prayed this prayer, and we can rejoice with you and help you achieve the destiny which God has for you!

Email us at vr@66Books.tv

Meet with other believers online at www.66Bible.Church

Bless you!

THE MISSION STATEMENT OF THE 66 BOOKS MINISTRY

WWW.66Books.tv | Our Mission is:

1. "To proclaim Jesus, the Savior of the whole world, from the whole Bible, because He is wonderful!"

2. Indeed, we are constrained by the love of God, to communicate the rawness of the Bible to real people, in real ways, and our driving and major project of '66Cities' shall take us to the 66 most influential cities of the 250 nations of the world in the next 25 years. That's 16,500 cities!

3. We are aiming to build relationships with grass roots, real people, that is, ordinary people, who, in their own countries and cities, want to do extraordinary things for Jesus and the Kingdom of God, to bring a Biblical Gospel message that is relevant to now, in a world that has come to believe that Jesus is irrelevant to their lives.

If you would like to partner with us in this great task. Then we want to hear from you! Contact me today on vr@66books.tv

MORE ABOUT 'THE 66 BOOKS MINISTRY'

WWW.66Cities.com | By the year 2047, by the grace of God and according to His will and favor, The 66 Books Ministry shall be preaching consecutively from each of the 66 Books of the Holy Bible, the Gospel of the Lord Jesus Christ in 16,500 of the most influential cities of the world on an annual and ongoing basis!

We do not underestimate the quality teams of trained people that this will take, together with the need for vast amount of materials and finances which will also have to be raised. However, as most futurists indicate that the growing global population will be gathered mostly in major world cities in the coming years, there is a necessity laid upon the church to present and proclaim the God of the whole Bible, through the primacy of preaching in these cities. We are convinced that this is a paramount and pressing concern.

"For since, in the wisdom of God, the world through wisdom did not know God, it pleased God through the foolishness of the message preached to save those who believe" 1 Corinthians 1:21NKJV

"Preach the Word! Be ready in season and out of season. Convince, rebuke, exhort, with all longsuffering and teaching." 2 Timothy 4:2NKJV

The church is looking for a revival. The 66 Books Ministry, however, is trying to start a revolution of a return to the preached Word, from the whole of the Bible as a precursor to any and all coming revival.

For "whoever calls on the name of the Lord shall be saved." How then shall they call on Him in whom they have not believed? And how shall they believe in Him of whom they have not heard? And how shall they hear without a preacher? And how shall they preach unless they are sent? As it is written: "How beautiful are the feet of those who preach the gospel of peace, Who bring glad tidings of good things!" Romans 10:13-15 NKJV

We are unashamedly looking for and seeking to foster a massive, huge, releasing, transformative, and exceptionally disruptive reversal and revolutionary change, both within the church and then in the world. We are not just another mission trying to do the same as every other mission. We are intent on revolution!

To this revolutionary end, we have no fear of seeming failure and will cultivate that audacious atmosphere within our ministry. We want to attract grass roots people who are people of faith risk takers, for we believe it is people of such life hazarding attitudes that are used by God to make breakthroughs in the world for the Kingdom of God. Hanging back for fear of seeming failure, hanging back and waiting for the trained professionals, both wastes the time of the church time and kills the spirit of victory.

In that spirit then, we therefore are believing that this task can be accomplished by such people within the time frame we have given ourselves.

Fully assured then, that we are in full obedience with the great commission of our great God and Savior Jesus Christ, we do, with great confidence in Him, turn ourselves happily to this so great a task in the hope that, like a happy hound straining at the leash to be let loose, we believe that many other people will smile along with us and be part of this brand new grass roots 21st Century Global City Mission.

If you want to know more and want to be part of what we are doing then go to www.The66BooksMinistry.com or call us in the USA on **855 662 6657**, or email V.R. directly on vr@66Books.TV

COMPILER BIO | VICTOR ROBERT FARRELL

WWW.VictorRobert.tv | Victor Robert Farrell (1960-Now & still alive and kicking) was born in Chesterfield England to Scottish parents with Irish grandparents, which is an obvious recipe for writing and emotional disaster, if ever there was one!

He grew up a culturally excluded Roman Catholic (his parents were divorced,) which is one of the reasons why he hates religion with a passion, and that's an interesting enough fact by itself, because he is also an ordained protestant minister to boot.

V.R. became a Christian whilst serving on board a Polaris Submarine at the end of the cold war. He has gone on to do many things, including being a broadcaster, App developer, performance poet, and the long-time author of 'Night Whispers,' which is read in over 100 counties and is also translated into Spanish (see www.Night Whispers.com)

Currently, V.R. is also President of The 66 Books Ministry: a grass roots global city mission endeavor. I suppose it is this concoction of background and experience which means V.R's communication is always raw and emotive. After all, "If Christianity can be relevant on a Monday morning, several hundred feet underneath an unknown ocean, in a pornographic sewer pipe carrying enough nuclear weapons to destroy a continent, whilst hiding from the Russians, then it can be relevant anywhere and everywhere!"

V.R. sees himself as a servant of the Word of the Lord, and communicating the God of the whole Bible, proclaimed in very real terms, to real people, is both his burden and his passion.

MORNING | MINOR PROPHETS

BOOK 38 of 66 | Zechariah 11

Signpost Words | 'EGGS OF THE SHEPHERD CLOWNS'

Highlight Verses | Zechariah 11:15-17

And the Lord said to me, "Next, take for yourself the implements of a foolish shepherd. For indeed I will raise up a shepherd in the land who will not care for those who are cut off, nor seek the young, nor heal those that are broken, nor feed those that still stand. But he will eat the flesh of the fat and tear their hooves in pieces. "Woe to the worthless shepherd, Who leaves the flock! A sword shall be against his arm And against his right eye; His arm shall completely wither, And his right eye shall be totally blinded." NKJV

Some Observations |

This chapter speaks of Christ the good shepherd, and finishes with hireling idiots! When Christ was rejected by Israel of old, they got Clown-shepherd hirelings to help them into hell. It is the same today.

Final Reflections |

In this magnificent and prophetic chapter God finishes by asking Zach to dress like a Clown-Shepherd? What does a Clown-Shepherd look like? He has a goatee instead of a full beard. He has his shirt hanging out over his backside. He has a perpetual goofy grin. He is rich, but he has no bread. He cannot heal nor bind up and therefore, he also has no balm from Gilead. He has no rod, and is followed by undisciplined sheep. He has no staff, but in its place a stool. What does a Clown-Shepherd look like? Well, look around Christian, there are many examples to choose from, and each one has an egg with their own garish face painted upon it. Why are we shepherded by Clowns? Because Christ has vomited Laodicea out of His mouth.

THE FELLOWSHIP OF THE BOOK

EVENING | MINOR PROPHETS

BOOK 38 of 66 | Zechariah 12

Signpost Words | 'THE CRIME SCENE OF THE CROSS'

Highlight Verses | Zechariah 12:10-14

"And I will pour on the house of David and on the inhabitants of Jerusalem the Spirit of grace and supplication; then they will look on Me whom they pierced. Yes, they will mourn for Him as one mourns for his only son, and grieve for Him as one grieves for a firstborn. In that day there shall be a great mourning in Jerusalem, like the mourning at Hadad Rimmon in the plain of Megiddo. And the land shall mourn, every family by itself: the family of the house of David by itself, and their wives by themselves; the family of the house of Nathan by itself, and their wives by themselves; the family of the house of Levi by itself, and their wives by themselves; the family of Shimei by itself, and their wives by themselves; ... NKJV

Some Observations |

So, Jerusalem shall be sieged once more and all nations shall come against the Jews. Then Christ shall come and both strengthen their hands and destroy all their enemies for them. At that point, Israel shall see the nail pierced hands of their Messiah, whom they crucified. Then, they shall repent and believe, and be saved! Amen!

Final Reflections |

National repentance is made up of broken individuals. Repentance might have a national expression, but in each case, it is of a very singular act. Christian, it is your sin which nailed your Savior to the cross. You have blasphemed Him. You have deserted Him. You have thrust the spear into His side. You denied Him. You despised Him, you used Him & you abused Him. You were at the crime scene of the cross. He remembers seeing you there! Be sure you remember Him dying there for you, so that He might remember you in His Kingdom.

JOIN THE FELLOWSHIP OF THE BOOK

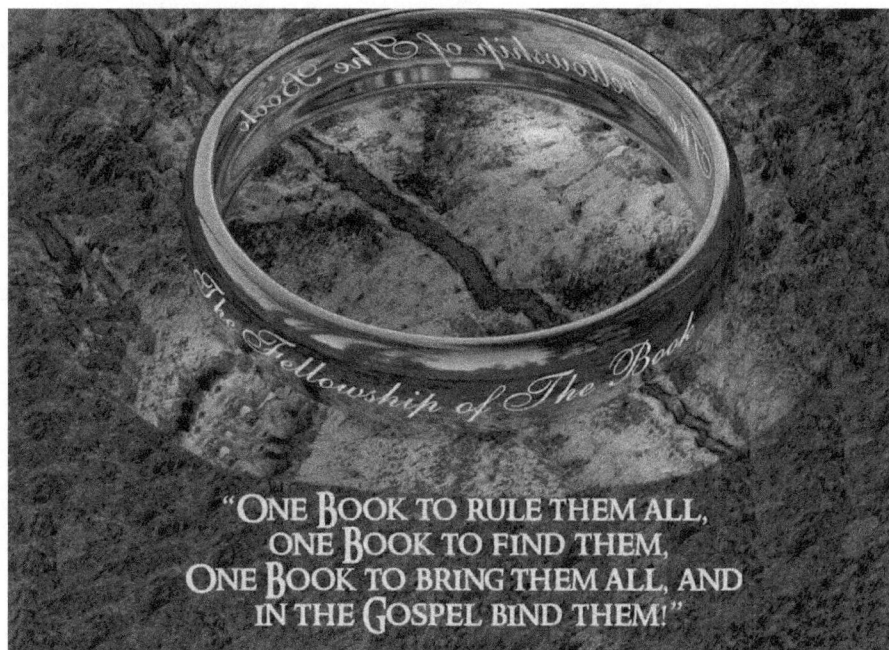

"ONE BOOK TO RULE THEM ALL,
ONE BOOK TO FIND THEM,
ONE BOOK TO BRING THEM ALL, AND
IN THE GOSPEL BIND THEM!"

WWW.TheFellowShipofTheBook.com

The Fellowship of The Book is a Daily Bible Reading Fellowship. You can sign up today and also PRE-ORDER this 738 page Book of 366 Daily Bible Readings with accompanying notes, divided as

Signpost Words
Highlight Verses
Some Observations
Final Reflections

Read The Bible Thru in 1 year, with a Morning and Evening reading to keep your mind focused on the Lord of the Word and the Word of The Lord. Buy this and several other 'Read the Bible Thru in a Year Books' at WWW.TheologyShop.com

ANOTHER BOOK BY THE COMPILER, VICTOR ROBERT FARRELL

Habakkuk A Prophecy For Our Time

As the Church in the West is found to be mostly dead and covered with Laodicean lukewarm vomit, as The Lord, slips the dead things silently over the side of the storm tossed ship into the dark oblivion of the waves of secular humanism and rising Islam, what remains will need to be fortified with steel to live in a quickly changing anti-Christian world of persecution. There is no better prophecy more equipped to speak to such a remnant who shall be so very besieged. Welcome to Habakkuk, 35 of 66, a prophecy for our time.

Buy at WWW.TheologyShop.com

ANOTHER BOOK BY THE COMPILER, VICTOR ROBERT FARRELL

The 66-Minute Bible

I am told that there are 788,258 words in the King James Bible and of these 14,565 are unique. That's a lot of words! I have been reading the Bible for nearly forty years on an almost daily basis. It still remains to me the most exciting book on the planet, however, it never gets any easier. Bible reading is a spiritual discipline and for me the emphasis is on discipline. I created this resource to aid you in your Bible reading, it gives your brain a sixty second overview of the Bible, a loose enclosure to herd the narrative of the book into something that can be seen as a whole. It was never created to be a substitute, but an aid. Just saying...... Friends, welcome to the most exciting book on the planet! V.R.

Buy at WWW.TheologyShop.com

AN INTRODUCTION TO 'PURPLE ROBERT'

Some Dangerously Different Devotionals!

Now, before I go any further, this guy comes with warning shots! The opening parts of his currently seven volumes pf poetic works says quite clearly, *"If you are easily offended by low level expletives...**Go no further. Do not read this book!** If you are prudish in any way ...**Go no further. Do not read this book!** If you do not want to be challenged...**Go no further. Do not read this book!** If you want to be stroked into unchanging sleep and into the stupor of remaining as you are...**Go no further. Do not read this book!** If you hide under the respectable covers of a comfortable religion...**Go no further. Do not read this book!** If you are frail in faith and dishonest about life under this sun...**Go no further.** If you have no real integrity regarding the state of your own heart, **then do not read this book!** If however, you are grown up, honest and have a basic human integrity,   ENJOY!"* So, there you go, you have been warned!

Purple Robert is a Performance Poet and a Metaphysical Biblical Realist. If you want to hear some of his work and get hold of the 66 Poems each of the Seven volumes contain, then go to www.PurpleRobert.com and purchase them today.

Also Buy at Buy at www.TheologyShop.com

www.ingramcontent.com/pod-product-compliance
Lightning Source LLC
Chambersburg PA
CBHW021212020426
42331CB00003B/327